Wensley Clarkson is an investigative journalist who has written numerous non-fiction books, screenplays and television documentaries. His books have sold more than a million copies in 17 countries worldwide.

HITMEN

HITMEN

TRUE STORIES OF STREET EXECUTIONS

WENSLEY CLARKSON

JOHN BLAKE

Published by John Blake Publishing Ltd,
3, Bramber Court, 2 Bramber Road,
London W14 9PB, England

www.blake.co.uk

First published in paperback in 2005

ISBN 184454 119 3

British Library Cataloguing-in-Publication Data:

A catalogue record for this book is available from the British Library.

Design by www.envydesign.co.uk

Printed in Great Britain by Bookmarque Ltd, Croydon, Surrey

1 3 5 7 9 10 8 6 4 2

© Text copyright Wensley Clarkson, 2005

Papers used by John Blake Publishing are natural, recyclable products made from
wood grown in sustainable forests. The manufacturing processes conform to the
environmental regulations of the country of origin.

Every attempt has been made to contact the relevant copyright-holders, but some
were unobtainable. We would be grateful if the appropriate people could contact us.

CONTENTS

Of all classes of killer the contract killer must be regarded as the worst; a man who is prepared to offer his services, to take the life of someone who is totally unknown to him and do it for payment.

RECORDER OF LONDON, SIR LAWRENCE VERNEY

INTRODUCTION

The number of hitmen on our streets today has reached epidemic proportions. Twenty years ago there was only a small crew of highly professional killers for hire carrying out a handful of hits. Yet by the beginning of the new century, there were more than one hundred paid-for murders in Britain each year.

But you wouldn't always guess it by reading the nation's newspapers. Professional hits get little coverage. As Fleet Street crime hack Peter Wilson says, 'One villain knocking off another doesn't have the same news appeal as a beautiful brunette blasting her cheating hubby to death.'

Genuinely professional hitmen revel in the low-key nature of their business. Says one, 'The less publicity the better. The papers don't seem that interested in most hits. The biggest coverage I ever got was a few lines in the *Standard*.'

In the past, even the police played down hits on criminals.

As one retired detective recently explained: 'We took the attitude that every time there was a hit that meant one less villain on the streets – and that can't be a bad thing.'

But now even the force's finest admit the situation has got out of control. Scotland Yard has a special secret squad to investigate these criminal renegades. David Veness, assistant commissioner in charge of specialist operations, admits, 'We have a genuine fear that there is a greater capacity for criminals to gain access to individuals willing to kill for money. There are worrying signs that there are small groups for whom this is the main form of criminal activity.' That's copspeak for 'It's a big problem.'

The bottom line is that life's a lot cheaper now than it was when sawn-off shotgun-toting armed robbers swaggered across pavements taking pot shots at *The Sweeney*'s John Thaw and Dennis Waterman as they crouched behind their Ford Granada. 'A lot of it's down to puff, E and coke,' says south-east London criminal Gordon McShane. 'Many of the robbers of the Seventies are now dealing drugs big time. We're talkin' about millions of quid changing hands. That means the rotten apples need to be dealt with. There's no shortage of work for a decent shootist.'

But who are they?

THE PROFESSIONALS

These are the characters who come up through the ranks to become professional hitmen. Their so-called skills are known to the country's most powerful underworld gangsters. They keep a low profile and tend to live anonymous, almost 'normal' lives. They also tend to only hit other criminals and avoid the high-profile jobs that end up in the tabloids. These pros thrive on the fact that their line of work is low profile and often hold down more respectable 'careers' within the traditional criminal fraternity. Many are so low-key it's virtually impossible for police to prove a link between them and the murders they have committed.

YARDIES

There is a smack-crazed posse of West Indian gangsters who dispose of rivals and, sometimes, their families with cold-blooded, execution-style killings that serve as a warning to anyone who dares to double-cross them in drug deals. Often their hitmen target rival drug dealers, rip off their produce and then wipe them out. As a final calling card they have been known to sexually assault their victims, whether male or female. In June and July 1998, the Yardies carried out three barbaric murders, including the execution of two young mothers. Scotland Yard linked the slayings after forensic tests revealed the victims were shot with the same 9mm self-loading handgun.

TRIADS

This gang, with its sickening brand of maiming and killing rival gang members, has been operating on Britain's streets for the past 30 years. But most of these murders go unreported – and unsolved – because of the Triads' Mafia-style secrecy and the fears of those within the Chinese community. Four main Triad societies, the

14K, We On Lok, Wo Shing Wo and San Yee On, rake in vast profits from protection rackets, prostitution, fraud, illegal immigration and illicit gambling. The Triads train up their own hitmen by importing previously unknown individuals from the Chinese mainland.

THE OPPORTUNISTS/SEMI-PROS

These are small-time hoods prepared to knock off other villains, cheating lovers and work rivals. They underprice the pros and are often desperate for cash to feed a drug or drink habit. One recent classic example of this was when the shooter intended to hit a little boy's stepfather who'd double-crossed local drug lords – instead the youngster was shot dead. These hitmen are more often caught because they don't think through the science of being a hired killer and take necessary precautions. And, chillingly, some of them are mere teenagers prepared to kill for a few hundred pounds.

These categories are just the tip of the iceberg. The cold, hard reality is that hitmen can come from every type of background and, as this book will show, they share one common factor: an appalling lack of regard for human life.

Wensley Clarkson 2005

Chapter One:

SPARKY

Maori Te Rangimaria Ngarimu's face had the bone structure of a warrior but she possessed the body of a beautiful young woman. Her lovers all praised her sensuous nature and her fondness for steamy sex, and her bubbly personality helped land her the nickname 'Sparky'. Te was 24 years old, confident, well educated – with a double first from a university back in New Zealand – and enjoying her life in Britain so much that she planned to stay for at least the next five years.

But Sparky's shapely body was well hidden by the baggy black tracksuit, sunglasses and baseball cap she wore in May 1992, as she strolled into the Royal Free Hospital in Hampstead, north London, to visit a sick friend. Sparky managed a typically pleasant smile at the nurse who kindly directed her towards the main men's ward.

Sparky calmly pressed the lift button as she waited

alongside a mother with her young child and two elderly women. Once inside the elevator she pressed number three, turned and glanced casually at the other visitors as the lift slowly rose to the third floor. When the doors opened she slid her hand into her handbag to check on the contents.

Then Sparky walked out into the corridor, and looked to her right and left before recognising the man she'd come to see. He was leaning casually up against a wall with a phone virtually glued to her ear while he talked quietly into the receiver. As Sparky began walking towards him, he turned his back to her, but she already knew for sure it was him. She'd studied his photograph closely the previous week and then followed him from his home to make sure she knew exactly what he looked like in the flesh. Sparky walked right past him as he continued talking into the phone. Another ten yards and Sparky casually turned around for one last glance.

Then she reached into her handbag and kept her hand buried inside it as she strolled back towards where he was standing. But just then something stopped her, she turned away and walked back towards the lifts, still grappling in her handbag. She firmly pushed the button to call the lift. Her target was just three feet from her. Now was the perfect moment. She flicked the safety catch on the gun in her handbag.

Graeme Woodhatch only noticed Sparky as she pulled the .22 pistol from her bag and aimed it straight at him, holding the weapon with both hands. His mouth fell open and started to move as she squeezed the trigger. His scream was drowned out by the explosion. Woodhatch tried to cover his face with his hands as the first bullet smashed into the centre of his forehead, another ricocheted off his backbone and severed an artery, a third demolished the bridge of his nose and the fourth embedded itself in his shoulder.

'Something just snapped inside and I did it,' Sparky later recalled. 'There were four shots but I remember pulling the trigger only once. That first shot hit him in the face – he was facing towards me. I do not remember firing the other shots, although I heard four. I remember seeing him rolling around on the floor screaming. He had his hands on his face.'

By the time Sparky had fired that fourth and final bullet, her victim already lay dead on the floor of the hospital corridor. She'd just earned £7,000 from Woodhatch's business colleagues for gunning down their enemy.

As Sparky glanced down at her victim one last time a man appeared from the other end of the hospital corridor. But before he could get too close, the elevator doors opened and Sparky slipped into the lift. Less than two minutes later, she hailed a passing black cab and headed back to an apartment owned by the man who'd commissioned the hit.

Half an hour later, Sparky let herself into the flat, grabbed a kitchen towel and began wiping her prints from the .22 gun. Then she stripped naked and placed all her clothes in a large black plastic bag before barking at her accomplice, 'Get rid of this shit as soon as poss.' That man must have felt the strangest combination of sexual excitement, fear and trepidation. She was riding high on adrenaline.

Sparky was what police later described as a 'semi-pro': she had knowledge of either firearms or violence, but was not a full-time criminal. More often than not semi-pros are unreliable and botch the job. They are frequently employed in domestic rows, to get rid of an awkward spouse or to sort out a business disagreement once and for all.

Sparky's only kill as Britain's first ever hitwoman would never have happened if she hadn't encountered two friendly men at a pub where she worked in north London. Paul Tubbs, 34, from Enfield, north London and New Zealand-born Keith Bridges – nicknamed Charlotte – 21, from Camden, also in north London, both fancied the attractive Maori who was always dressed in figure-hugging jeans and tight, slinky blouses. Tubbs and Bridges ran a roofing firm with Graeme Woodhatch and believed that Woodhatch was swindling the company out of thousands of pounds.

At the pub where Sparky worked, she quickly formed a close bond with her fellow countryman Bridges. He even let her stay in a room in his flat and the two new friends were soon pouring out all their troubles to each other. Sparky, a chemistry graduate and national sportswoman, played hockey, surfed and spoke fluent Japanese so she was interesting company.

Sparky told Bridges she'd been a master shot back in New Zealand and that her dream was to save enough money to buy her own home when she eventually returned to New Zealand. Bridges told Sparky he had big problems at work and explained how Graeme Woodhatch was endangering everything that he and his partner Tubbs had worked for over the years. During one chat, Bridges even mentioned 'knocking him [Woodhatch] off'. Then he asked, 'Would you do it, Sparky, for a certain amount?'

'Yeah, I'll do it,' she replied at double-quick speed. Neither of them seemed emotionally capable of questioning the severity of what they were proposing.

A few days later, Bridges provided Sparky with a photograph of her intended victim so she could identify him for the hit.

'And where is he now?' asked Sparky.

'He's at home but he's going into hospital next week to have an operation on his piles,' responded a deadpan Bridges.

'Has he got any kids?' asked Sparky, ignoring the fact her intended victim was about to go into hospital.

'Nope.'

Sparky later insisted, 'I would have thought more about it if he'd had children.'

'Charlotte' Bridges advised Sparky that if she was caught she should make out Graeme Woodhatch had done something really bad to her. 'Charlotte promised he'd come to visit me in prison,' Sparky later recalled.

Over the next few days, Sparky stalked her intended victim just to make sure she knew exactly what he looked like when the day came for her to murder him.

Then Bridges provided Sparky with a .22 pistol – known across the middle of America as a 'Saturday Night Special' on account of its cheapness and availability to the good citizens of the most powerful nation on earth. Sparky showed off her knowledge of such weapons by opting to use hollow-tipped bullets for maximum damage. Bridges informed her that Woodhatch had just gone to hospital for his operation and it would be the perfect location for the intended hit.

'Buy a hat, gloves and some tracksuit bottoms so you don't stick out in a crowd,' Bridges said. Being mistaken for a man would be a big advantage in the aftermath of the killing. In any case, no one would believe a woman could carry out such a heinous crime.

'Shoot him twice in the head and twice in the chest just to make sure,' advised Bridges. He then rather tactlessly admitted that his business partner Paul Tubbs was paying him a total of £10,000 to get rid of Woodhatch – £7,000 of which would be passed on to Sparky. He was keeping the rest as commission.

So it was that Sparky set off for the Royal Free in search of Graeme Woodhatch. Minutes after getting to the hospital she abandoned the hit because she couldn't find the correct ward. She might also have been suffering from a bout of cold feet.

Next morning, when he heard about her aborted mission, Keith Bridges began putting some serious pressure on Sparky. 'Just think about the house bus [mobile home].' As she later explained: 'I had always wanted one – it was going to be my home. It cost $30,000 [£10,000] back home. I thought about it all the time. It was my goal in life.'

A few hours later Sparky returned to the hospital and shot Graeme Woodhatch dead before heading back to Keith Bridges' flat.

Back at the Royal Free, medical staff hadn't even realised that Graeme Woodhatch had been shot because no one had actually witnessed the hit, and the bullets from the .22 were so tiny that doctors believed his wounds were the result of a fall in the corridor. Only after resuscitation attempts had failed and the dead man's girlfriend had departed having spent four hours with his body, did staff preparing the corpse for the mortuary become suspicious of his facial injuries. They noticed what looked like bullet wounds.

John Cooper, chief executive of the Royal Free, defended his staff's extraordinary oversight. 'Very experienced British medical and nursing staff may well never have seen a gunshot wound of the kind suffered by Mr Woodhatch,' he said. 'Some types of gunshot wound appear as no more than discolouration of the skin around a puncture mark. The entry-exit wound from a gunshot may be very small and may not bleed.'

But as one police officer later pointed out: 'If we'd realised earlier that a man had been assassinated inside the hospital we would have been on the trail of the killer much more quickly.'

At one level the hit on Graeme Woodhatch seemed incredibly amateurish. Yet Sparky had a definite lucky streak; she was able to walk out of the building virtually unchallenged because no one realised Woodhatch had been shot.

Also, there had been no eyewitnesses. There were 12 lifts near where the killing occurred, plus two fire escapes. There were even three public exits from different parts of the hospital. How on earth were detectives going to establish whether the killer had been seen by anyone?

Detectives initially described the shooting as a 'criminally professional' operation. As one firearms expert explained: 'Whoever did this job knew what they were about – two shots to the head and two to the body to make certain of a kill, plus the clever choice of weapon. It is easily available, it fits in the palm of your hand, it is no louder than a cap gun, and it does the job.'

Thirty miles away, to the south of London, Sparky was checking in at London's Gatwick Airport for a 4.30pm flight back to New Zealand. She was pulling out her ticket to check the details when she found that photo of the victim still in her pocket. It was the first time she realised the full enormity of what she'd done. She left the check-in line, walked into the nearest ladies' lavatory and ripped the photo into tiny shreds before flushing it down the toilet.

Then she tore off every item of clothing she was wearing, including her black G-string. Sweat was dripping off her body and she was shaking like a leaf. All those earlier feelings of excitement had been replaced by fear combined with a severe dose of paranoia. For a few moments Sparky stood stark naked in the toilet cubicle in the departure area of Gatwick, wondering how on earth she'd just managed to kill a complete stranger. A rap on the door from another female passenger waiting snapped her out of her momentary feeling of self-doubt. Sparky slipped on a pair of tight black leather trousers, buttoned up a fresh blouse and marched out of the ladies with her head full of strange thoughts and emotions.

Back in north London, Graeme Woodhatch's colleague Paul Tubbs telephoned a friend and arranged for him to pick up a holdall containing the murder weapon from Keith Bridges. The bag also contained bullets, the baseball cap and other clothing worn by Sparky for the hit. The following day it was all thrown into a lake.

Less than 48 hours later, Sparky turned up on the doorstep of one of her closest friends in New Zealand. Within a week, paymaster Keith Bridges had sent her newspaper cuttings about the murder plus a money order for £1,500. The contract killing of a hospital patient had made front-page news in the UK but there was no suggestion the murder had been committed by a woman. One newspaper reported that Woodhatch had wanted to leave hospital early, after his beautiful 26-year-old Israeli girlfriend told him she was pregnant. That left Sparky feeling a tad guilty, so she tore that cutting into pieces.

Then British newspapers began investigating the background of victim Graeme Woodhatch and uncovered a string of business debts totalling almost £1 million from his roofing firm. Even Woodhatch's former brother-in-law said the dead man had made a lot of enemies in his business dealings. Newspapers reported that Woodhatch drove top-of-the-range sports cars, including a Porche 911, took lavish holidays and was never short of a pretty girl on his arm. And it emerged that, two days after his death, Woodhatch himself had been due to appear in court in Clerkenwell. He'd been accused of threatening to kill 22-year-old Emma Harrison, a secretary working for his company. All those revelations helped convince Sparky that justice had been done.

North London detectives had also been busy looking into the dead man's business associates and put Keith Bridges and Paul Tubbs at the top of their suspects list. Officers had deliberately cast a wide net of suspicion by publicly suggesting Woodhatch had hoodwinked numerous people and that it was inevitable someone would want to do him harm. Detectives went as far as to describe Woodhatch as 'a

Maxwell without the brains' after the late, little-lamented and deeply dubious publishing mogul Robert Maxwell.

Paul Tubbs even agreed to be interviewed by newspapers. He told one reporter: 'Within a week of employing Graeme he was getting personal threats on my phone from people he owed money to.'

Then detectives established that Keith Bridges had been sharing his flat with a mysterious Maori woman who'd disappeared back to New Zealand on the same day as the killing. At first, officers found it difficult to contemplate that a female could have carried out such a cold-blooded killing. Then they heard about her experience with guns. A team of Met Police detectives were immediately dispatched for New Zealand.

A few days later, London detectives confronted Ngarimu in New Zealand but she denied all knowledge of the killing. She even looked the officers in the eye and told them she couldn't have carried out such a shooting because she was a vegetarian and 'could not even kill a chicken'. After three visits to her home, the detectives travelled back to London empty-handed. They did not have enough evidence to charge Sparky.

But a few days after that visit by British police, Sparky found herself walking past a church in New Zealand and felt herself drawn inside. There she began having second thoughts about what she'd done. Shortly afterwards, her sister gave her a Bible which she read over the following two weeks. Afterwards, she announced to friends that she'd 'found the Lord'. She also felt increasingly guilty about killing Graeme Woodhatch.

Sparky then got a call from her local police to say that Keith Bridges and Paul Tubbs had been charged in connection with the Woodhatch murder back in London. That development had a profound effect on Sparky. Within hours she'd called the police back and agreed to return voluntarily to London to face murder charges. As the prosecutor of the case later explained: 'It was a matter of conscience and living with her actions. It is an unusual situation for a murderer to return from abroad, to acknowledge her responsibility and guilt, to co-operate and be prepared to give evidence. She was at the very heart of the conspiracy.'

Sparky was officially arrested when her plane from New Zealand touched down at Gatwick Airport and she was charged with murder later that evening at a north London police station. Newspapers labelled her Britain's first female contract killer. At Sparky's first court appearance in front of Hampstead magistrates in north London she was tense, distraught and full of remorse.

Paul Tubbs and Keith Bridges were unaware that Sparky's conscience and conversion to God had influenced her decision to plead guilty to the Woodhatch murder and turn Queen's evidence against the men who hired her.

In May 1994, Sparky appeared at the Old Bailey and pleaded guilty to murdering Graeme Woodhatch. Oliver Blunt, QC, told the court that Sparky's conversion to Christianity was complete and she was even attending Bible classes three times a week at Holloway Prison as well as attending church services every Sunday. She was also teaching autistic children in the prison gym. Blunt told the

Old Bailey: 'She knows that beyond my Lord's sentence, she faces the judgements of her Lord.'

Recorder of London, Lawrence Verney, told Sparky: 'You have pleaded guilty to the most terrible offence that can be committed, the taking of the life of a fellow human being in circumstances which are a disgrace to you. The obvious motive was the payment of money and the act was carried out in cold blood.' He then sentenced her to life in prison.

The judge said he would normally make a recommendation that 'someone employed to kill' should serve a minimum sentence in excess of 20 years. However, because Sparky had given evidence against the two men behind the murder, he would be more lenient, he said. He even acknowledged that Sparky had turned over a new leaf and would not be carrying out any more hits. He said, 'I am satisfied that you are not a professional killer. You have expressed deep remorse and I accept that, but it is not a fact which can have very much influence on my recommendation to the Home Secretary [regarding the sentence].'

Later that same month – May 1994 – the trial of Bridges and Tubbs was delayed after Bridges was mysteriously shot in the chest while out on bail. As a result, he was left disabled with a partially paralysed arm. His lawyer told the court that Bridges had been the target of an assassination attempt.

The trial of the two men finally went ahead in December 1994 and, on 17 December, a jury at the Old Bailey found Bridges and Tubbs guilty of conspiracy to murder. Both showed little emotion as the jury delivered their verdict, following a deliberation of more than 12 hours. Each man was given a life sentence. Recorder of London, Sir Lawrence

Verney, recommended that Bridges should serve a minimum of 15 years and Tubbs a minimum of 16. Both men had earlier admitted to perverting the course of justice by disposing of the gun Sparky used for the hit and were given three-year sentences to run concurrently with their life sentences.

Chapter Two:

THE BERMUDA TRIANGLE

'**B**ig Al' Decabral squeezed his 22-stone frame into the
driver's seat of his son's Peugeot with great difficulty.
He was more used to touring his manor in his own vintage Jag
– once owned by Reggie Kray – or his even bigger Rolls-
Royce. He didn't even notice the car pulling up alongside him
as he checked the time – 1.37pm – on his gold Rolex in the
car park of a Halfords store in Ashford, Kent. So when the
driver aimed a gun at him he only had time to mutter the
words, 'Please don't shoot me,' before two shots rang out and
40-year-old Decabral's vast body slumped against the
Peugeot's steering wheel.

Shoppers at the nearby Sainsbury's and Curry's fled as the
killer ran off. Seconds later Decabral's 20-year-old son walked
out of Halfords to find his father dead. He collapsed to the
floor sobbing, 'My dad's dead, my dad's dead.'

Welcome to Kent – the Garden of England – on Thursday, 5 October 2000. Just beyond Halfords were rolling fields of golden corn, converted millhouses and luscious green pastures. It's supposed to be the ideal of what the countryside should be: peaceful, winding country lanes filled with modest folk minding their own business, motivated by a love of gardening; certainly nothing as vulgar as money or hitmen. But lurking in among the unprepossessing villages of Kent are many of the major names in the British underworld and Big Al Decabral had just paid the ultimate price for daring to take on the big boys.

One of the few witnesses to the Decabral killing was 26-year-old Anton Kaye, deputy manager of the nearby Curry's store at the same shopping centre. He said, 'He [Big Al] was sat with his head slumped slightly to the right on the wheel. He was wearing sunglasses and looked about 50. There were no doors open and no signs of broken glass, so the killer obviously got up pretty close to him.'

Within seven minutes of the killing, police were examining a silver, H-reg Mercedes parked 35 yards from the dead man's car, which they believed belonged to the hitman. Police cordoned off the murder scene and the surrounding area as forensic teams searched for clues. Officers did not let anyone leave the busy retail park and then announced: 'We're hunting a man who was seen running from the scene wearing a light green jacket and is described as being in his early twenties. We are appealing for shoppers who may have visited the retail park to contact us.'

Big Al's former wife told reporters: 'I'm devastated. I just feel numb with shock.'

The truth was that heavyweight 'entrepreneur' Alan Decabral knew his days were numbered. Just three months earlier, the father-of-three had given evidence at a high-profile Old Bailey trial about how he'd seen so-called master criminal Kenneth Noye stabbing a motorist called Stephen Cameron during a road-rage incident on the M25 in 1996. Whether that decision sealed his fate we'll probably never know, but it's worth considering.

Even Big Al admitted that the moment Noye's name came into the frame for the Cameron killing he was warned not to give evidence against him. Decabral's name was even mysteriously leaked to the press before the trial. Kent Police told Decabral that a civilian in the typing pool at their headquarters had sold the information to a newspaper. Shortly afterwards, it was even alleged that Decabral was contacted by one of Kenny Noye's numerous associates and warned that his decision to help police could cost him dearly.

At a meeting a couple of days after his name was blasted across the newspapers, it was even alleged that Decabral was told: 'Either shut up or you'll be permanently silenced.'

Decabral later said defiantly, 'I don't like being told what to do. I'm very stubborn when pushed. I don't like being ordered around.'

A week after that incident, Decabral found three bullets lying on the hall carpet of his home. He later explained: 'Somebody was telling me not to testify. I was a bit freaked out by it.' But he didn't tell police what had happened.

Before giving evidence against Kenny Noye at the Old Bailey in the summer of 2000, Decabral was snubbed by numerous old friends and associates in Kent. 'I'd go into a pub I'd been going in for years and people would shuffle away from me. Then I'd shout at them, "I'm doing this for the right reasons."'

But then Kenny Noye was – and still is – one of the richest and most powerful criminals in Britain. Handling the proceeds of huge drug deals and bank robberies has helped make him tens of millions of pounds. He's a member of that exclusive gentlemen gangsters' club: the Brinks-Mat team. That legendary robbery at Heathrow Airport in 1983 has linked many of Britain's most powerful criminals.

When Kenny Noye appeared at the Old Bailey in the summer of 2000, after he had pulled a knife out from under the front seat of his car and killed motorist Stephen Cameron on the M25 roundabout, he claimed he was simply defending himself. Then Big Al Decabral told the court he saw Noye commit the murder. Noye stared intently at the overweight, unhealthy-looking Decabral as he struggled with his massive frame into the witness box.

He told the Old Bailey how he saw Noye's knife: 'I saw a flash. I could see the sun glinting off the blade.' Then he told the court: 'As he [Noye] went past my car he just nodded at me and the expression was as if to say: "That's sorted him out" or "You've got yours, mate."'

Minutes later there were gasps of surprise in the Old Bailey when a tape of a 999 call Decabral made after seeing the killing was played. It featured clear references to Decabral's work and home telephone numbers as well as his home address for anyone to note down. Many believe that is when the clock really started ticking for the countdown to the end of Big Al's life.

The Old Bailey jury eventually found Noye guilty of murder by a verdict of 11–1. Lord Chief Justice Latham told Noye: 'The jury having found you guilty of murder, there is only one sentence I can impose and that is one of life imprisonment.'

After the trial, Big Al admitted to one friend, 'Seeing Stephen's murder changed things. I thought, What if it had been my son? I got told by lots of people, "You shouldn't say anything. It's Kenny Noye." But that doesn't change things. I am no angel but I do have certain standards. I did what I thought was best. The consequences have been worse than I'd ever imagined, but I would still do it again.'

Cut to three months later and Big Al is lying dead in a car park.

Within 24 hours of the Decabral hit, Kenny Noye was telling associates he was furious that his name had been linked to the killing. Detectives insisted they had no clear idea of the identity of the killer or who might have commissioned the hit. From his cell in Whitemoor Prison, Cambridgeshire, Noye implied that the claims were a deliberate slur to try and damage his attempts to appeal against his sentence. Kent's Detective Inspector Bob Nelson told journalists: 'The more we investigate this crime, the more complicated it becomes. The public and the media should not jump to conclusions.'

Incarcerated Kenny Noye insisted on seeing his two sons Kevin and Brett, plus his loyal long-time lawyer Henry Milner, to discuss how best to respond to the numerous newspaper stories linking him to the killing. Meanwhile all the other important witnesses who gave evidence against Noye at his trial were offered tighter police protection just in case they were in danger.

To this day, Noye remains in a special secure unit and is categorised as 'an exceptionally high-risk Category A' inmate. He's considered to have the financial and logistical means to mount an escape bid. Prison Service sources insist that to date Noye has been a model prisoner. He is not allowed to leave the unit to mix with other inmates or to use other facilities, including workshops and education classes. On every visit by friends and family he's separated from them by bullet-proof glass.

There is absolutely no concrete evidence linking Kenny Noye to the hitman killing of Big Al Decabral on 5 October 2000. But many had told Decabral to expect the worst and 'watch yer back'. Despite that, Big Al even turned down full police protection because he knew he'd never be able to continue his own criminal activities with police officers constantly looking over his shoulder.

Yet Big Al knew his life was at risk from the moment he appeared in the witness stand at the Old Bailey. He even admitted to one friend: 'I look over my shoulder every time I go to Sainsbury's.'

Eight weeks before he was killed, he received a series of new telephone death threats but police failed to establish a link between those threats and Kenny Noye. And one Kent detective described Decabral thus: 'This guy wasn't Mother Theresa, there were any number of people who had a grudge against him.' Others let it be known that Big Alan Decabral had links with numerous criminal activities including drug deals, gun-running and smuggling. 'He mixed with a lot of unsavoury people, any one of whom might have wanted him out of the way,' said another police source at the time.

After his death, Big Al's ex-wife Marie even backed the police claims by insisting Noye 'had nothing to do with it. Alan had so many enemies it could be any number of people. Somebody else has finished him off.' Marie and the couple's two children Charlotte, 12, and Dean, 8, stood to inherit the bulk of Decabral's supposed £6 million fortune, which included 14 luxury cars, motorbikes, jewellery and furniture as well as properties in Marbella and Pluckeley, in Kent.

Ex-wife Marie then publicly announced she was prepared to give evidence on Noye's behalf at his appeal saying that her husband had lied in court. She told one newspaper that Decabral had 'embellished' his story in a bid to stop police investigating his own criminal activities. 'I know people will hate me for saying this but everyone deserves the right to a fair trial – even Kenneth Noye,' said Marie. 'I believe he did wrong and should be in prison for killing that poor boy Stephen Cameron but I don't think it was premeditated. I don't think he got out of the car thinking, I am going to murder him.'

At the time of Noye's Old Bailey trial, Decabral had told the court he followed Noye in his Rolls-Royce as he fled the murder scene, and even wrote down Noye's registration number. 'That was rubbish,' said Marie. 'He was driving away from the scene because he didn't want to be stopped by police. Alan had been on his way to Lewes, East Sussex, to drop off a consignment of cocaine. He told me he used the car chase as an excuse because he feared being arrested.'

Marie also said that Decabral lied at Noye's trial when he

claimed he was only a 'recreational' user of drugs. She said, 'He was a big-time dealer and his use of cocaine got so bad that he had nose bleeds all the time.' Marie then revealed that just two days after Decabral had given a full interview to one British newspaper following the Noye trial, she received a chilling phone call from her estranged husband.

'I was outside my son's school waiting to pick him up when the mobile phone rang, and it was Alan. I said, "What are you playing at?" And he said, "I can kill you now, bitch. Everybody will think it's Kenny Noye."' Marie Decabral then wrote a letter to Kenny Noye in Whitemoor Prison. 'I wanted Noye to know the truth,' she said. 'But I also reasoned that if he needed my help he would not hurt us.' Two weeks later, on 3 August 1990, Marie took a call on her mobile phone. 'Hi, I'm Kevin Noye, Kenny's son,' said a male voice.

'I nearly dropped the phone,' Marie later recalled. They arranged to meet 30 minutes later outside a McDonalds in Eltham, south-east London. 'I was so nervous that Kevin said he could tell it was me from 20 yards away. We sat in his car and he asked me what information I had and why I wrote to his dad. I told him that Alan had lied under oath and he asked if I could prove this. I said, "Yes."' Marie claimed she also told Kenny Noye's 30-year-old son that she was 'very scared' of his father. He responded, 'Why would my father want to harm you?'

Meanwhile the trail for Decabral's killers went totally cold. An inquest into his murder the following summer of 2001 returned a verdict of unlawful killing. As Detective Chief Inspector Bob Nelson said at the time, 'We have failed to accumulate enough evidence to get the perpetrator.'

But the legend of master criminal Kenny Noye continues. There were even rumours that he was innocent of the road-rage murder of young motorist Stephen Cameron. Others say he's so well connected with detectives in south-east London and Kent that he helped to get the Stephen Lawrence suspects out of police custody after making one phone call.

But the gunning down of Big Al Decabral in broad daylight in Kent by that lone shootist sent shockwaves through the south-east London underworld and police. Noye has friends and enemies on both sides of the fence, and most were asking how Decabral could have been presented at the Old Bailey as the prosecution's star witness in the murder trial of Kenneth Noye.

Noye's world is filled with death, drugs, robbery and gold bullion. Yet he has spent much of his time living openly in palatial splendour, right slap-bang in the middle of Kent. But the death of seedy, obese Big Al provoked a minefield of questions – some of which might end up helping Noye win his appeal against his life sentence for the murder of motorist Stephen Cameron.

The key to Big Al's assasination probably lies in a vast area of Kent countryside stretching from Noye's favourite village of West Kingsdown past Biggin Hill – and its handy airstrip – across to Swanley. It's known to Kent detectives and villains as 'The Bermuda Triangle'. As one senior police officer explained: 'Things that go in there have a habit of never coming out again. And we're talking about everything from people to lorryloads of bootlegged fags 'n' booze.'

The construction of the nearby M25 has meant easy access to the Bermuda Triangle at all times of the day and night. And it was on the Swanley intersection of the M25 that Alan Decabral insisted he saw Kenneth Noye kill Stephen Cameron in May 1996. One Kent detective summed up the police attitude when he told me: 'I can guarantee that if there were 20 vehicles on that M25 roundabout at the time of the Cameron killing then at least five of those drivers would be known to us as villains.'

A coincidence? Or was Decabral put up as a star witness at Noye's Old Bailey trial to ensure that Noye – who once knifed an undercover police officer to death in his garden and was later acquitted of murder – wouldn't get away with another killing? If Noye and Decabral did know each other before the Cameron murder was committed, why wasn't it more openly revealed during Noye's trial?

And would Noye – as many were quick to claim in the wake of the Decabral shooting – be obsessive (or stupid) enough to commission a hitman to so publicly execute a witness in his trial when he was intending to present himself in an appeal as a victim of some appalling injustice?

Noye knows full well that Decabral's previously undisclosed criminal connections would have worked much better for him if he was still alive. As ex-Detective Chief Superintendent Nick Biddiss, who led the early stages of the hunt for Noye, said after the Decabral killing, 'If Noye was responsible, he shot himself in the foot. If he was going to do it he should have done it before the trial. If he was behind it now he could not have timed it worse because of his appeal.'

Some faces in the badlands of south-east London and Kent reckon it's more likely that one of Noye's loyal cronies paid for the Decabral hit out of respect for Noye, forgetting about the importance of his appeal. Others believe Decabral's killer was paid by Noye's enemies, determined to make sure Noye would be blamed and his appeal would be left in ruins.

Another story doing the rounds is that Noye ran up so many debts while on the run from police following the Cameron killing that a group of his angry associates commissioned the shooting. 'Think about it,' one underworld contact said to me. 'It makes total sense. And it would explain why the execution was carried out in broad daylight. They was sending a message to Noye.' It's certainly true that Decabral had so many enemies of his own that they might have ordered the hit knowing that Noye would get the blame. Another popular theory is that Decabral took a £100,000 bribe to agree to water down his Old Bailey evidence, but then reneged on the deal and gave such a damning account that it guaranteed Noye would be jailed for life. 'Whatever the truth a lot of people are going to have to watch their backs – and I'm talking about police and villains,' says one who should know.

It can also be revealed now, for the first time, that Decabral boasted of meeting Noye at a number of gangland parties before the Cameron killing in May 1996. 'If this is true it totally throws into question his validity as a witness in a murder trial,' explained one criminal lawyer. Other criminals insist Noye and Big Al were well acquainted.

Kent Police – who masterminded the prosecution of Kenneth Noye – claim they already knew about Decabral's criminal background but Noye's lawyers made no attempt to probe it in open court. However, days after Decabral offered his evidence to police, a team of Kent detectives raided

Decabral's home looking for drugs. They found a stash of guns and took away £150,000 in cash which they later returned untouched. All charges against him were dropped when the officers realised Decabral was an important witness in the upcoming Noye trial. The police who prosecuted Noye have always claimed they knew nothing about that alleged raid on Decabral's home. As one retired detective told me: 'How could one group of officers in the Kent Constabulary not know about the raids carried out on Decabral's house?'

Part of the answer may lie in some of the intriguing developments that occurred in the run-up to Noye's Old Bailey trial. One ex-Kent detective who followed the proceedings closely explained, 'I heard there was some wheeler-dealing behind the scenes.'

The result of this 'wheeler-dealing' was that Noye's representatives hammered out an agreement in an effort to ensure Noye would not face a mandatory minimum sentence after being found guilty of the Cameron killing. As one ex-Kent detective explained: 'It's like the wild west out there. There are some outlaws in south-east London who are a law unto themselves. If they've got a problem with the cozzers [police] there's always someone they can call to sort things out.'

A spectre has hung over police in Kent and their neighbours in the Met ever since Kenneth Noye first started greasing palms back in the early Seventies. Noye even joined a Freemason's lodge in west London to get nearer to 'the enemy'. Noye already boasted of a circle of acquaintances that crossed all social divides and included several Kent magistrates. Noye also cashed in on the policeman's favourite philosophy that 'a good detective is only as good as his informants. And a copper's informants, by their very nature, are going to be villains or associates of villains.'

The problem with this philosophy is that it leaves detectives wide open to accusations of corruption. Criminals, like Kenny Noye, have happily helped police in an effort to divert attention from their own activities while at the same time obtaining, through the usefulness of the information given, a degree of protection from prosecution.

And Kenny Noye's activities have also never been inhibited by incarceration in Her Majesty's Prisons. At one stage in the late Eighties he was purchasing shipments of ecstasy pills in Amsterdam through a fellow inmate inside Swaleside Prison, in Kent. That inmate was bodybuilding drug dealer Pat Tate who later died in the notorious Essex Range Rover killings when three criminals were shot dead in a field in December 1995. Now I can reveal for the first time that another one of Pat Tate's 'clients' was Alan Decabral. Yet more evidence of connections between Noye and the man who was murdered in a car park after he'd given evidence against Noye.

In the mid Eighties, multi-million-pound drug deals took over from security van robberies as the number one source of income. Dozens of upwardly mobile druglords, money launderers and handlers of stolen property turned the Kent countryside into their premier destination and they spent a lot of out-of-pocket expenses on keeping certain members of the local constabulary happy.

Step forward Alan Decabral – once a renowned drug dealer in Acton, west London – now looking for pastures new and a bit of peace and tranquillity in the Kent countryside. He, like

Noye and dozens of others before him, was attracted by the idea that it was 'much more tricky to shadow a villain down a deserted country lane than a busy London street'.

At the other end of the county, the Channel ports of Dover and Folkestone provided the gateway to Europe and all its highly lucrative drug-trafficking routes. One retired bank robber has made a small fortune running villains such as Noye and Decabral from a tiny port near Dover across to Holland where drug barons head off for 'company meetings' in Amsterdam. 'You can get in and out of Europe without the cozzers knowing anything about your movements,' explains retired cannabis smuggler Gordon Scott. 'The fella who runs it has this tasty motor launch complete with bedrooms and a fully stocked bar. He'll even bring on the dancing girls if you book well in advance.'

Another of Noye's one-time neighbours who no doubt crossed paths with Decabral was John 'Little Legs' Lloyd. He recently returned to his detached home after a five-year stretch in one of Her Majesty's Prisons. One south-east London source told me: 'I've heard that Decabral used to boast about his connections to Lloyd. There's no way that Kenny Noye didn't know all about him.' There are quite a disturbing number of Kenneth Noye's associates who've met violent ends. Decabral came across many of them at the Kent gangsters' parties he boasted about regularly attending.

On 1 April 1998, the UK's first National Crime Squad was set up by the Government to combat the growing menace of organised crime. The unit's launch was directly linked to the newly installed Labour government's dissatisfaction with the way that criminals like Kenneth Noye and Alan Decabral had been able to increase their activities and continue to live openly in luxurious surroundings.

Not surprisingly, many of Kent's most infamous 'faces' were among the top targets. National Crime Squad chief Roy Penrose even insisted at the time: 'We will be targeting criminals who are the most difficult, the most prolific and the most lucrative. There is no hiding place. We will use every legitimate method to track them down.'

Police in south-east London still believe that other villains in the area were 'queuing up' to pull the trigger for their hero, Kenny Noye. 'The money paid for the job is almost insignificant against the brutal kudos to be gained from being "the man" to blow away the chief prosecution witness against Noye,' explained one detective. 'The killer would have respect and forever be owed a favour by Noye. You cannot underestimate Noye's continuing influence in the underworld because of his access to untold wealth.'

Kenny Noye's appeal against his conviction was dismissed, but a later appeal against his life sentence was accepted and it was reduced to a minimum 16 years. The mystery of who commissioned the hit on Big Al Decabral remains to this day.

Chapter Three:

SWIMMING WITH SHARKS

The Lincolnshire village of Uffington (population 530) lies just a few miles from the ancient market town of Stamford, the setting for the BBC TV series *Middlemarch*. Most of its houses are occupied by wealthy, middle-class professionals: businessmen, lawyers, accountants and officers from nearby RAF Wittering. Estate agents use words such as 'idyllic', 'picturesque' and 'tranquil' to describe Uffington.

Resident Diane Emerson-Hawley seemed the perfect example of the sort of glamorous blonde that the village welcomed into the fold. Diane and her new husband Colin Harrold moved into their £400,000 home – set in half an acre of grounds and screened from the road by a tree-lined garden and driveway – in the first few weeks of 1999. Mr Harrold had originally trained as an engineer but now ran a printing business and a separate enterprise selling recycled books for use as pet bedding. The couple, both divorcees, had first met on a blind date and married in 1997. Mr Harrold had two sons aged six and ten by his first wife.

At the back of the property – called Barn House – was an impressive-sized swimming pool where Diane liked to keep fit most mornings before she drove her sports car with personalised number plates to the beauty salon she owned in nearby Stamford. Diane and Colin often went jet-skiing or took Colin's powerboat out at weekends. Thirty-six-year-old Diane was known as a down-to-earth, warm and generous lady without an enemy in the world. A lot of that attitude came from having started her working life as a low-paid casualty nurse who'd sacrificed her youth to look after her sick mother. Diane had certainly packed a lot into her life.

In the middle of October 1999, Colin Harrold flew to Amsterdam on one of his regular business trips. The following day, when his wife did not answer the phone at their home, he contacted his brother, Neil, who lived locally.

Neil went to the house and found the back door wide open and no sign of a break-in. In the couple's bedroom a wardrobe had been ripped open and Colin Harrold's clothes were scattered everywhere. A nearby door that led to the loft was slightly ajar. It appeared that someone had been frantically searching through the house. Neil Harrold then noticed a trail of blood from the kitchen towards the front door. He immediately left the house and ran to the local pub, Ye Olde Bertie Arms, arriving at 7.45pm 'in a very distressed state'. He asked to use the telephone to contact the police.

Officers arriving at Barn House found Diane Harrold's

body floating fully clothed, face down in her outdoor swimming pool. The couple's home was immediately cordoned off by police. It appeared Diane had first been attacked in the kitchen and then dragged outside. A tap in the sink was still running when police arrived at the scene and a bottle of washing-up liquid lay on the floor where it had fallen during some sort of struggle.

Detectives concluded that Diane must have still been alive, though possibly unconscious, when she was hauled outside and thrown into the water. Her killer had left a chilling 'calling card': the body of Diane's beloved pet cat was floating in the pool beside her. Investigators also found that a substantial amount of cash was missing. But with no sign of a forced entry there wasn't a clear motive for the murder.

Meanwhile husband Colin Harrold flew home from Amsterdam and went to stay with friends. As Diane's father-in-law later told reporters: 'If I could have picked a daughter from anyone in the world, it would have been her and I know Colin loved her very much.' Everyone was in an understandable state of shock.

The news of Diane Harrold's violent murder sparked a series of lurid headlines in newspapers across Britain. There were rumours of a vendetta against her beauty salon. One year earlier she'd bought the Cameo Health and Beauty Salon in Stamford and had been struggling to make it work. Then all the windows were smashed and she was also plagued by a series of strange phone calls, including bogus bookings and cancellations. Lorraine Rose, who ran the nearby Poppies dress shop, later explained: 'The girls in the salon were scared by all the strange phone calls and cancellations. They knew something was not right but we never imagined something like this could happen.'

Back in Uffington, residents were understandably stunned by the murder. 'Diane was a terribly nice person and there has never been a cross word about her in the village. How does someone so nice come to an end like this?' asked one neighbour.

Police appealed through the media for help in tracing Diane's movements between 3pm on Tuesday, when she was last seen alive, and Wednesday evening when her body was found. As Detective Superintendent Chris Cook pointed out: 'It is likely that the offender will be bloodstained and I would appeal to anyone who has any suspicions regarding any relation, friend, neighbour or associate to get in touch.'

Then investigators began unravelling the life of Diane and Colin Harrold. It emerged that they'd met through a lonely hearts advert placed in the *Peterborough Evening Telegraph* newspaper. For Diane, it had been love at first sight and friends admitted she was much more keen to get married than he was. Two years after their wedding – in early 1999 – Colin Harrold told his best friend Darren Lake that Diane was 'bleeding him dry' of money. Lake later recalled, 'He said Diane wanted children, which he did not. He wanted his freedom.' Lake and Harrold had met many years earlier when they were both apprentices at an engineering firm.

At the point when he got married for the second time, Harrold's speciality was buying thousands of end-of-line books from publishers for a few pence a title, claiming they were to be shredded. In fact, police discovered he'd then sell them on to shops at home and abroad, making massive tax-free profits. He claimed he even bribed officials at book companies to turn a blind eye. 'People were looked after,' Harrold later said. 'It was a win-win situation all the way down the line.' Many of the deals were in cash and he planned to set up bank accounts in Malta to avoid tax.

Police soon established that Harrold pocketed at least £100,000 of undeclared income each year. A further import-export line in hard-core sex magazines – described in court as 'commodities' – was his next venture. Colin Harrold's crafty wheeler-dealings were beginning to make him look like a possible suspect in the murder of his wife.

Detectives retracing Colin Harrold's footsteps while he was away on his 'business trip' in Amsterdam discovered he'd frequented the city's notorious red-light district after he'd phoned his brother to check up on why Diane had not been answering her phone at home. Was his role as a caring, loving husband all a charade?

Then Harrold's former wife Annette told police that two weeks before Diane's death, Harrold told her he was having an affair with another woman and that he was in love with her. Annette later recalled, 'Knowing how we parted over money I said to him that it would cost him dearly. He said to me, "I'm already working on it."'

Annette Harrold also told police that after Diane's death her former husband insisted his new wife had been murdered during a burglary but then made a point of saying she wasn't to worry about the safety of their children. Up to this point, police had deliberately not yet revealed that they knew there hadn't been a break-in.

Then it emerged that, the month before Diane was

murdered, Colin Harrold booked into a health farm in Leicestershire with his latest mistress, Tania McCarter. They spent much of the day together in a whirlpool bath and steam room. Harrold later admitted to police that they'd had a 'touch and feel' session. But Ms McCarter insisted they did not have full sex and that – shortly before Diane was murdered – she'd finished her relationship with Harrold because he was married.

Then one of Diane's oldest school friends told police she'd noticed the couple arguing when she stayed with them two months before Diane's murder. Joanne Hewitt said, 'It was tetchy. There were arguments. Diane had everything apart from what she really wanted, which was children. She made a lot of overtures about wanting children. But he said he didn't want children.'

Another woman called Kim Milne met Harrold and his best friend Darren Lake on a night out with friends in a bar in Peterborough. During a conversation she asked Harrold if he was married. Harrold answered, 'I've been married for two years. Two years too bloody long. Money is changing hands as we speak. I am doing something about it.'

Police believed that whoever committed the murder expected detectives to accept that Diane Harrold had slipped and fallen into the pool by accident after trying to find her cat, Cleo. But among the bloodstains in the house was a shopping bag smeared with a handprint which they believed came from the killer. And one of the names that kept coming up during police enquiries was Harrold's best friend Darren Lake. Harrold's friends and associates said the two men were very close. Lake eventually agreed to have his fingerprints taken. Investigators were astounded to find that it was Lake's handprint on that plastic bag.

On 12 November 1999, Colin Harrold and 30-year-old Darren Lake were arrested in connection with the murder of Diane Harrold. Lake had been best man at Harrold's marriage to his first wife Annette. Harrold was taken into custody by police at a house in Peterborough and held with Lake at Boston Police Station in Lincolnshire. A white Vauxhall Astra belonging to Lake was also taken away for forensic examination.

Colin Harrold's ex-wife Annette then told reporters from her home in nearby Yaxley, Lincolnshire: 'I have been praying this wouldn't happen for the sake of the children. I am horrified – but not shocked.' She later told one newspaper how she'd once arrived home early to find Harrold dressed in her clothes. She also claimed he was obsessed with both gay and straight pornography.

Back in the sleepy community of Uffington, Harrold's arrest for murdering his wife astonished the locals. Retired farmer and neighbour John Conington said, 'I am flabbergasted by the news of Colin Harrold's arrest. That anything like this could happen in our village is almost unthinkable.'

Shortly after the arrests, detectives uncovered a letter Darren Lake had written to his father in which he claimed that he himself might be Harrold's 'next target'. The letter said, 'There will be one of three reasons for my death: No 1 – natural or accidental death. No 2 – a man hates me and has it in his head that I have slept with his girlfriend. No 3 – this is probably the real reason for my death: Colin Harrold has probably either paid for my hit or killed me himself.'

Shortly after the letter emerged, Lake confessed to his part in the murder to police and alleged he'd been paid £20,000 to kill Diane Harrold.

Colin Harrold made his first court appearance following his arrest in a ten-minute hearing. He was on crutches following a sporting accident in the Nottingham prison where he was being held. His best man Darren Lake later wept in court as the charges against him were read out.

In July 2000, Nottingham Crown Court was told that Colin Harrold, who'd already begun an affair with another woman, had decided it would be too expensive to divorce his wife so he'd have her murdered instead. James Hunt QC, prosecuting, told the court: 'This man, Colin Harrold, had a wife, Diane. She was his second wife. She wanted children. He did not. Moreover, he became tired of her and was playing with another woman. He had a lot of money and lived a lavish lifestyle. It would have been expensive to divorce his second wife and she would know too much of his shady business to be bought off cheaply. He therefore arranged a contract with a friend, named Darren Lake.' QC Hunt continued, 'This case is not a whodunnit. We know whodunnit. Darren Lake has admitted it. It is a question of who got him to do it. We say that it is plain. That it was Colin Harrold. Although items in the house were disturbed, it was plain that it was not a burglary.'

Lake initially told the court he'd worked as Harrold's 'gofer' for £30 a day and the businessman had even lent him

£2,000 to buy a car. Then, a month before Diane's murder, Harrold offered to write off the loan and pay him a further £18,000 to get rid of his wife.

Lake recalled, 'We were in his office having a coffee and he said, "I have a proposition for you. I'll give you £20,000 to knock off Diana." I was shocked. He then put his hand in his pocket and brought out a photograph. It was a picture of me on holiday ten years ago when I was about 20. It was in Tenerife, our first trip abroad.'

Lake said the photo showed him being raped by three men, on the beach at Playa de las Americas. He insisted to the jury that he didn't know who took it. Lake claimed Harrold then said that unless Lake carried out the killing, copies would be sent to his father, his fiancée and a former girlfriend, the mother of his seven-year-old son. Lake insisted that his 'whole world caved in' when he was shown the picture by Harrold, who had kept it for ten years.

Lake told the court: 'With Colin you don't say "no". I never said yes – it was just expected.' He went on, 'He said it would be easy – easy, no problem. "Just knock her on the head and put her in the pool and make it look like an accident."'

Lake even recalled how he set about committing the murder which they both codenamed 'Cleo' after Diane Harrold's cat. When Diane returned home from work that evening, Lake said he sat chatting with her on the sofa before producing a wooden post and hitting her over the head with it: 'There was blood everywhere inside the house,' he told the hushed court. Then Lake said he pushed Diane Harrold's body into the water, returning several times to ensure that she had not climbed out. Lake was then asked by QC James

Hunt, 'How could you do such a thing?' Lake looked across at Harrold and said, 'I was frightened of him.'

One of Colin Harrold's cellmates even took the witness stand and claimed that the businessman had confessed to the killing while in jail awaiting trial. John Bond, 44, explained: 'He told me he left the money for the hit in the house, and Lake made it look like a break-in.'

When Colin Harrold finally took the witness stand he insisted he was 'very much in love' with his brutally murdered wife. Harrold told the court she was 'the centre platform of my life'. He added, 'We were soulmates, very close and intimate.'

Harrold admitted cheating on his wife but insisted he never had full sex with mistress Tania McCarter. He said, 'I had plenty of sex at home.'

There was a hushed silence at Nottingham Crown Court when the jury returned their verdict on Colin Harrold. Harrold swayed and grasped the bar of the dock as the jury gave a unanimous verdict, finding him not guilty of the murder of his wife.

Less than an hour later, the same trial judge Mr Justice Moreland said Harrold's best friend Darren Lake's evidence was 'probably, essentially truthful'. Moreland told the 31-year-old former nightclub bouncer: 'You were the actual cold-blooded and merciless planned murderer of a woman who, seconds before you attacked her, was treating you as a friend and with whom you falsely pretended to be friendly. It is however to your credit that you have pleaded guilty and, at risk to your own life, have given evidence for the Crown.'

As Colin Harrold walked free from Nottingham Crown

Court and returned to the same £400,000 house where his wife was murdered, his only words to the waiting packs of journalists were: 'I am relieved.'

Meanwhile Detective Chief Superintendent Chris Cook, who'd led the investigation, said, 'We placed the facts and circumstances surrounding the case before the court and now, quite obviously, we must abide by the decision of the jury.' The jury's verdict had effectively rejected the prosecution's case that Colin Harrold wanted Diane dead so he would be free to continue his playboy lifestyle.

Colin Harrold inherited his dead wife's share of their £400,000 home just one year after her murder. Harrold was also named as chief beneficiary in Diane Harrold's will which meant he inherited her £30,000 estate, apart from some jewellery, which went to her brother. He also got more than £100,000 in legal aid because on paper he claimed to be virtually penniless at the time of his arrest and subsequent trial. There were also rumours that he'd sold his life story to a national newspaper for £40,000.

On the first anniversary of his wife's murder, Colin Harrold was to be found hand-in-hand with his so-called 'former mistress' Tania McCarter. The couple were photographed frolicking on a beach in Israel. Harrold had been so paranoid about being spotted in the company of Ms McCarter that they'd flown out to Tel Aviv on separate flights from the UK. One former friend said, 'What they are doing is disgusting. What came out in the trial would have shamed most men into keeping their head down. It's almost as if he's dancing on Diane's grave.'

Meanwhile some of Diane's relatives spent that same anniversary in Scunthorpe, where they placed flowers on Diane Harrold's grave. One said, 'He appears to have chosen to commemorate the anniversary in a slightly different way. The brass neck of the man is incredible.'

After his controversial acquittal, Colin Harrold sold his dead wife's beauty salon business and also came to an 'arrangement' with the Inland Revenue over unpaid taxes. A couple of his few remaining friends even claimed he'd also spent £4,000 on liposuction of his flabby midriff.

Harrold made an appearance on his local radio station to assure people that they should not be scared of him. 'It's important that people are aware of what I am about so they are not worried if they pass me in the street.' During the hour-long interview with a local radio station in Peterborough, he spoke of his 'shock' at his arrest. 'I was inside for 10 months. My grief was day and night all the time I was there. For someone to say this guy doesn't care about Diane, his wife, is just crazy.'

After hearing Harrold's interview on the radio, Diane's brother, Darren Hawley, commented, 'What he has said is very interesting. I used to believe that Colin Harrold was a nice person, but I don't think he is fooling anyone any more.'

So Colin Harrold continues to live a life of luxury in the house where his wife was so cruelly bludgeoned to death and then drowned by his best friend. 'I've got absolutely nothing to hide. Why should I leave the area where my family lives? I have done absolutely nothing wrong.'

Chapter Four:

THE MOTHER-IN-LAW FROM HELL

Elizabeth Duncan proves that a mother's love for her son can be so strong that it sparks murder and mayhem. But then Hazel Sinclara Nigh – as she was born in Kansas City in 1904 – was building up to a life of crime and notoriety from the moment she adopted the Christian name Elizabeth and married her first husband Dewey Tessier, when she was just 14 years old.

Elizabeth had three children by him, but they were all soon dispatched to the nearest orphanage because her skills as a mother left a lot to be desired, although the same could not be said of her ability to seduce men. Elizabeth would eventually marry at least a dozen other men. Many of those marriages were bigamous, and most of the bizarre unions were swiftly annulled on the grounds of non-consummation, although Elizabeth was a deft hand at blackmailing her long list of hubbies into making healthy-sized cash support payments.

Elizabeth's other big speciality was defrauding gullible businessmen by luring them into so-called honeytraps in hotel rooms with young girls and then embarrassing them into making large one-off payments to avoid the local constabulary. Elizabeth was certainly a one-off.

In 1928, she married yet another sucker of a man called Frank Low. Just four months later a boy called Frank Jnr was born. Low died in 1932 – a year earlier Elizabeth had moved on to to another, wealthier bedmate called 'Mr Duncan' whom she'd married bigamously before Frank Low's untimely death. Elizabeth was to use the name Duncan for much of the rest of her life although she also occasionally used the surname 'Craig' after another of her marriage partners. That name came in particularly handy during fraudulent financial transactions because Mr Craig had a very good credit rating.

Meanwhile, baby son Frank Jnr became the only consistent presence in Elizabeth's ever-changing life. She proudly took the infant everywhere with her, even to the brothel she helped run, not to mention numerous bars and clip joints where little Frank often found himself sitting in Elizabeth's Chevy Rambler automobile sucking on a bottle of soda while his mother went about her business.

It wasn't long until another husband – a kindly old fellow called George Satriano – came on the scene. He showered Elizabeth with gifts and the couple moved into a huge mansion on the edge of town. Then George began noticing a few discrepancies in his bank account. He withdrew her credit cards and dropped her monthly allowance to a few dollars.

Elizabeth was so outraged she picked up the yellow pages

and found herself a private detective, whom she offered $500 to throw acid in her husband's face for daring to question her honesty. Fortunately for George, that little plot came to nothing, but few could blame him for filing for divorce. He was so grateful to escape the marriage with most of his fortune still intact that he agreed to give Elizabeth his brand new Cadillac as part of a settlement.

Naturally, Elizabeth had been out looking for a new husband even before her divorce from George Satriano was finalised. She needed funds to put her beloved son Frank through his law studies in San Francisco so she set up a brothel in Santa Barbara, a very civilised beach resort halfway between LA and San Francisco. She called it a massage parlour and persuaded a handsome young stud called Benjamin Cogbill to be her partner in business and in bed.

But Ben couldn't keep pace with Elizabeth's frenetic lifestyle and he was soon shown the bedroom door. A swift stroll down the church aisle with 26-year-old Stephen Gillis followed, after Elizabeth promised Gillis $50,000 if he'd marry her. Her latest toyboy just happened to be one of her beloved son Frank's classmates at law school. Elizabeth insisted the $50,000 was the proceeds of a non-existent trust fund. But the nearest handsome young Stephen got to any of that cash was a cheque for $10,000 which bounced its way out of every bank in the state.

The only fortunate aspect of that wedding for Stephen Gillis was that the marriage wasn't consummated. He somehow managed to avoid living with the now frumpy, middle-aged and seriously overweight Elizabeth. However, when he asked for a divorce, she accused him of assault, fraud and blackmail – enough damaging claims to ruin his plans to be a lawyer. Stephen Gillis eventually fled his battles with Elizabeth to join the Marines. She was furious that he'd rather join the toughest training unit in the world than stay with her.

Days after Gillis's departure, Elizabeth marched into a local doctor's surgery with a pregnant woman in tow. She introduced the young woman as Mrs Elizabeth Gillis and the doctor confirmed her pregnancy. Gillis was then forced to send baby support money to her before he could finally win an annulment of their marriage. As Gillis later admitted: 'She had a tremendous spell on everybody that she came in contact with, and no matter what lie she told, no matter how fantastic, it was believeable.'

Back in the rich and glamorous Pacific coastal resort of Santa Barbara, Elizabeth continued running her brothel and supporting her beloved son Frank. Her immaculate dress and good manners gave the impression she was rich. But behind her quaint horn-rimmed glasses those piercing blue eyes and her thin mouth told another, chilling story.

Everything took second place to her beloved son Frank who even admitted to his friends and colleagues that he was 'the apple of my mother's eye'. But that bond between mother and son took a disturbing twist after Frank qualified as a lawyer. Elizabeth soon made it her business to be in court whenever Frank was working. She loudly applauded his speeches and even rushed across to hold her son's hand adoringly whenever there was a break in proceedings. But worse still, Elizabeth would berate the District Attorney if Frank lost a case. None of this helped Frank, especially since he was already known in local legal circles as the 'Wicked Wascal Wabbit' on account of his distinct lisp.

And back at their house in Santa Barbara, Elizabeth and Frank continued to share a bed. One of her oldest friends later recalled, 'She said that sometimes she'd call to Frankie and that he'd come and jump in bed with her and console her or she'd go and jump in Frankie's bed.' Frank later denied that any such activities ever took place but by that time the damage had already been done.

Elizabeth adored taking centre stage at every gathering, especially with her group of elderly friends who seemed in awe of her razor sharp wit and pushy personality. One of her most adoring fans was a stony-faced widow in the first throes of senile dementia called Mrs Emma Short. One day she popped round to Elizabeth's house and was immediately shown 'Frankie's' bedroom. His mother cooed at her son as he lay asleep, 'Isn't he beautiful?' Elizabeth then described him as 'still Mama's little boy'. Frank was almost 30 years of age at the time.

Elizabeth Duncan openly admitted that she couldn't stand the thought that her beloved son might actually leave home one day. Once, when she suspected Frank was about to move into his own apartment, she swallowed back just enough sleeping pills to send out a customary 'cry for help' message. When the doctor treating her pointed out that her adult son Frank might one day get married and leave home, she snapped back, 'Frank would never leave me. He wouldn't dare. He wouldn't dare get married.' A few weeks later she told one friend that if Frank ever contemplated marrying, she would 'get rid of her'. That icy threat sent a shiver up her friend's spine.

In November 1957 Frank even dared stand up to his mother by insisting she could not afford to buy a beauty parlour in Santa Barbara. A bitter row erupted and Frank ordered his tearful mother out of their home.

Within hours, Elizabeth had thrown back yet another handful of sleeping tablets. She wanted him to feel sufficient guilt to allow her back into his life. Frank rushed to her bedside as she lay recovering from her ordeal in Santa Barbara's Cottage Hospital. Elizabeth purred with delight as Frank held her hand and begged for forgiveness.

Then into the ward walked attractive 29-year-old nurse called Olga Kupczyk, who'd moved to Santa Barbara the previous year from Vancouver, Canada, where her father had worked as a foreman on the railroad. She was a quiet, friendly girl without an enemy in the world.

Elizabeth Duncan watched with anger from her hospital bed as a romance blossomed between Olga and her beloved son. When Frank suffered a severe bout of flu a few days later Olga sent him a bunch of get-well roses. Elizabeth threw them straight in the bin. Not long afterwards, Elizabeth informed her elderly, demented cronie Mrs Emma Short that she would 'break that little bitch's legs' if she continued romancing her beloved son.

Frank tried to play down his relationship with Olga because he knew his mother was angry about it. Then, in May 1958, Olga told Frank she was pregnant. The expected backlash from Elizabeth was as predictable as a bag of sand in the Sahara. Initially, Frank only admitted to his mother he was contemplating marriage to Olga. Within minutes, Elizabeth had picked up the telephone and started raging at the pretty young nurse, 'I will kill you before you ever marry my son.'

Frank tried to calm her down by promising he wouldn't actually marry Olga without first giving Elizabeth some notice. But he went back on his word almost immediately by obtaining legal dispensation to marry Olga the following day. Frank couldn't face telling his mother the truth. She'd long since turned him into a coward.

The secrecy that surrounded Frank and Olga's wedding was more befitting a rock star than a mummy's boy with a bad lisp and an average career in law. Frank ensured there were no telltale announcements in the local press. But he avoided certain issues by continuing to live with his mother and pretending that nothing had happened. The young couple's romantic wedding night was interrupted when Frank got out of bed to return home to his domineering mother. As Frank later admitted, 'It was a nightmare. I was going back and forth like a yo-yo.' In many ways he only had himself to blame.

Frank had also completely misjudged his mother's cunningness. She'd known about the wedding within hours of the ceremony, after phoning the hospital to speak to Olga only to be told by another member of staff that Nurse Kupczyk was packing in her job because she'd just got married.

This was war. And there could only be one winner: Elizabeth Duncan.

Just four days after the wedding ceremony, Elizabeth mounted her first outright attack on the unfortunate Olga by placing an advert in the local newspaper. It stated that

Frank Duncan was not responsible for debts contracted by anybody other than his mother. When Frank spotted the notice he weakly begged his mother to keep her nose out of his business.

Next Elizabeth began harassing Olga every time she saw her in the street. She also persuaded local shopkeepers that Olga was in debt at nearby department stores and should not be given any credit. Elizabeth even telephoned Olga most days threatening, 'If you don't leave him alone, I'll kill you.'

But a few veiled threats were not enough to get rid of Olga. So Elizabeth recruited the help of her demented pal Mrs Emma Short and another Miss Marple clone, seamstress Helen Franklin. Together, this unlikely threesome hatched a plot to kidnap Frank and then 'drum some sense into the boy'. They were going to knock him out with sleeping pills, drive him to Los Angeles and then force him to sign the relevant divorce papers. A few days later, those two little old ladies, Mrs Short and Mrs Franklin, talked their way into Frank's apartment and tried to tie him up but he refused to co-operate and they ran out of the flat. Frank later laughed it all off as a practical joke.

Then Elizabeth got chatting to one of her less salubrious acquaintences, a local ex-convict called Ralph Winterstein, who'd been sent to clean her windows by the Salvation Army. Would he mind impersonating her son Frank in order to obtain an annulment of his marriage? Elizabeth convinced Winterstein that Frank couldn't go in person to the courts because he didn't want his professional reputation as a lawyer ruined by being spotted at the divorce court offices.

On 7 August 1958, Winterstein (posing as Frank),

Elizabeth Duncan (posing as Olga) and Emma Short (posing as Olga's aunt) went to an attorney's office in nearby Ventura County. The case was immediately scheduled for later that day. But when this unlikely threesome turned up in court, Sally Army man Winterstein broke down and admitted he was not Frank. He was later convicted of perjury and Elizabeth was spitting fire.

Olga was so worried by her unpredictable mother-in-law that she moved apartments twice but the obsessive Elizabeth Duncan tracked her down each time after following her beloved son Frank home from work. Elizabeth then insisted to one apartment block manager that Frank and Olga were 'living together in sin'. Elizabeth then went and ruined it all by ranting, 'She is not going to have him. I will kill her, if it's the last thing I do.'

Then Elizabeth and her doddery partner in crime, Emma Short, started discussing murder as if it was as normal as that day's weather forecast. Elizabeth concluded that her old favourite of throwing acid in Olga's face couldn't guarantee a fatality. Even with a badly burned face, Olga could prove a threat to Elizabeth's bid to win back her son. Another plan involved luring Olga into Emma Short's apartment where Elizabeth would be waiting with a rope. She'd leap out of a cupboard, strangle the nurse, then weigh her body down with rocks and hurl it into the nearby Pacific Ocean. Emma Short wasn't keen because she didn't want a corpse hanging in her neatly stacked closet for hours before they hauled it down to the beach. 'I'd never be able to get rid of the smell,' she said, with utter seriousness.

She approached another elderly neighbour called Barbara Reed to help 'take care' of Olga by throwing acid into her face before Elizabeth smothered Olga with a chloroformed blanket. Then Olga would be trussed up, driven to the mountains in Frank's car and thrown off a cliff. Elizabeth even offered to pay £1,500 to Mrs Reed for her assistance. Mrs Reed told her friend Elizabeth she'd think about it and then told Frank who immediately confronted his mother. Elizabeth naturally insisted that Barbara Reed was lying. For some bizarre reason, Frank believed her.

Elizabeth decided it would be better to hire someone else to do the dirty deed on her behalf so she began chatting up drifters in local lowlife bars and then offering them money to murder her daughter-in-law. Most of the men she approached thought she was high on drink or drugs and took little notice. Then Elizabeth remembered a woman called Diane Romero, whose husband Rudolph had been successfully defended on a drugs charge by her beloved son Frank. Elizabeth located Mrs Romero and pointed out that her and her son were owed a favour. She spun a yarn that Olga was blackmailing Frank and offered Mrs Romero $1,500 to visit Olga's apartment at 1114 Garden Street, Santa Barbara, and kill her. Mrs Romero reluctantly agreed to the hit. But the next day she knocked on Olga's door and was horrified to discover she'd once been a patient of Olga's back in British Columbia.

Mrs Romero made an excuse and retreated to the nearest payphone where she called Elizabeth and cancelled the hit. Then Mrs Romero's husband, Rudolph Romero, was approached by Elizabeth who offered him $2,000. He declined her kind offer and even ignored her threats to have him thrown back in jail. But he didn't bother telling the police about his strange encounter with Elizabeth Duncan.

On 12 November 1958, Elizabeth Duncan set off – with the demented Mrs Emma Short in tow – to the seedy side of Santa Barbara and a grubby beer house with the unlikely name of the Cafe Tropical. She'd heard of the tavern when Frank had defended owners Esperanza Esquivel and her husband Marciano on charges of receiving stolen goods. The case against Mrs Esquivel, an illegal Mexican immigrant, had been dismissed but Marciano had pleaded guilty and was awaiting sentencing at the time.

Elizabeth and her friend Mrs Emma Short strolled into the Cafe Tropical and ordered coffees as if they were sitting down to breakfast in a family diner. Elizabeth immediately introduced herself to Mrs Esquivel and told her she was Frank's mother. She claimed that Olga was blackmailing her and threatening to throw acid in her beloved Frank's face if he didn't give her money.

'You got any friends who'd help me get rid of her, perhaps get her out of the way?' Elizabeth asked in much the same way that most people would ask if they could have sugar in their coffee.

Mrs Esquivel's brows arched and she gave the question some thought. 'I know some boys, but I don't know if they'd talk to you or not.'

'Maybe I could meet them,' suggested Elizabeth in her finest sugary sweet tones.

'Come here tomorrow afternoon and they'll be here.'

At 2.45pm the following day, Elizabeth and her doddery

old friend Mrs Emma Short were introduced to two young Mexicans, 21-year-old Luis Moya Jnr and his best friend, 26-year-old Augustine Baldonado, known to all as Gus. Both were unemployed labourers who occasionally swept the floors of the Cafe Tropical in exchange for meals. Baldonado also lived with the Esquivels.

Moya, from the Mexican town of San Angelo, was a convicted burglar and desperate for money to feed his drug habit. Baldonaldo was similarly inclined, but neither had ever expressed a desire to kill someone for a fee.

As the quartet sat down, Mrs Esquivel did the introductions. 'This is Mrs Duncan. She wants to talk to you,' she said. Uneasy smiles were exchanged before the extremely nervous Mrs Emma Short was dispatched to a back table away from the negotiations.

'How much?' asked Moya.

'$3,000,' ventured Elizabeth as calmly as ever.

'Make it $6,000,' snapped Moya.

'You got a deal,' said Elizabeth. '$3,000 up front and the remainder after the job's done.'

'We need a car, weapons and gloves,' added Moya, who'd taken the role of official spokesman for the two would-be killers. 'We ain't got much dough so can we have somethin' right now?'

Elizabeth didn't trust them an inch but threw them a $100 bill before providing a list of other 'props' that might come in useful such as rope, sleeping pills and acid, which she already had from all those previous unsuccessful attempts on her daughter-in-law's life. Elizabeth also supplied the precise location of Olga's apartment and her work routine since Olga had returned to nursing at the nearby St Francis Hospital.

As Moya later explained: 'We all agreed that if we saw her coming or going from work and if there was nobody around, we'd kidnap her off the street, or go up to the apartment and have the door opened for us and force our way inside and perhaps knock her out or somethin' and then tie her up, get rid of all her clothes or part of her clothes and make it look like she was on vacation or something. Then we'd take her to San Diego and get her across the border into Mexico and do away with her in Tijuana.'

Elizabeth Duncan even pointed out at the time, 'You'd better watch out. She's a pretty strong girl. She might put up quite a fight.'

The two men looked blankly at Elizabeth. The strength of a mere woman was not something they'd lose any sleep over. Moya then blandly announced: 'I know where to get hold of a gun.'

He turned down Elizabeth's kind suggestion that they use her car to transport Olga to her grave. Even these two drifters knew it was better to make sure there were as few links to their employer as possible.

Shortly afterwards, Elizabeth left the Cafe Tropical and headed to the nearest pawn shop to raise the cash for the hitmen's first proper down payment. She traded in two rings for $175, which she gave to Moya in the kitchen of the cafe a few minutes later.

Elizabeth and the two young Mexicans even agreed on a code word – 'Dorothy' – to be used at all times. Elizabeth also mentioned she'd already wasted $1,000 on another hitman who'd let her down. Moya and Baldonado knew she meant business.

As Elizabeth and Mrs Emma Short tottered back out of the cafe, she turned to her elderly friend and said, 'I think we got a real bargain with those two.' But then Elizabeth had absolutely no intention of paying the two Mexican drifters another penny.

Moya never even suspected she'd renege on the deal. He later explained: 'We trusted Mrs Duncan. We reckoned her word was good, as we made good ours.' And Moya and Baldonado certainly kept to their side of the bargain. They hired a cream-coloured Chevrolet and borrowed a .22 pistol from a pal.

At 11.00pm on the evening of 17 November, Baldonado arrived at the cramped apartment of Moya's girlfriend Virginia Fierro and picked up his accomplice before they headed off to carry out the hit.

That evening Elizabeth's daughter-in-law Olga was entertaining two old nursing colleagues from the Cottage Hospital where she'd once worked. They left the apartment at around 11.10pm. Twenty minutes later the Mexican's cream-coloured Chevy rolled quietly up near the neat two-storey apartment block on Garden Street. Moya slipped silently up the stairs alone, leaving Baldonado slumped in the back seat.

When Luis Moya knocked on the door of number 1114, Olga answered wearing a skimpy pink dressing gown over her seven-months-pregnant belly. 'I brought your husband home, Señora,' he said in broken English. 'I met him in a bar and he's pretty drunk. He got a lotta money on him and told me to bring him home. He's downstairs in the car but I need help getting him up here.'

Although Frank rarely drank alcohol, Olga didn't question Moya any further. 'Sure, let's go get him,' she said.

She walked down to the pavement with Moya and saw what she thought was Frank slumped in the back seat.

'Frank?' she called quietly, not wishing to wake up the neighbours.

As she leaned in to take a closer look, Moya pulled out his gun and smashed it over the back of her head before bundling her into the back of the car, screaming. Just then the man in the back seat – Baldonado – sprang to life. As Moya raced round to the driver's seat, Baldonado held Olga down. But she continued screaming and struggling and even made a grab for the door handle. Baldonado tried to throttle her but she just wouldn't be silenced. At a set of traffic lights, Moya leaned back and smashed the gun butt into her head until she finally crumpled to the floor with blood pouring from her head. Soon they were heading out of town and south towards the Mexican border.

But then the ancient, rusting Chevy started shuddering and both men wondered if it would make the 250-mile trip to Mexico. The two hitmen decided to divert and head for the mountains just 30 miles south of Santa Barbara. As Moya later explained: 'We'd find a nice little spot to bury her in.'

That 'nice little spot' turned out to be a ditch just off Highway 150. But as the drifters pulled Olga's body out of the back of the Chevy she recovered consciousness. They couldn't shoot her because the gun had been broken during that earlier ferocious assault. So both men took it in turns to strangle Olga before grabbing a nearby rock to make absolutely sure she was dead this time. Baldonado even leaned down to check her pulse.

They intended to bury her, but had forgotten to bring a spade, so both of the hitmen began digging with their bare hands. It took almost four hours, but finally Olga's corpse was dumped in the hole. On the short drive back to Santa Barbara Baldonado blurted out the six-million dollar question: 'Let's hope the old lady pays up.'

'No problem, hombre,' replied Moya. 'She'll pay.'

The two men then screeched to a halt on the edge of town to rip the blood-splattered seat covers out of the car before returning it to the rental office. They told the company they'd got drunk the previous night and accidently started a fire with a cigarette. Then it was off to celebrate their big windfall by having a party with their few friends.

By early next day, Frank and Olga's friends were so worried by her disappearance that they called the police. And back on the sleazy side of Santa Barbara, Moya and Baldonado were expecting their payment. Moya called Elizabeth at her home and announced, 'We've done the job. When do we meet to collect the dough?'

Elizabeth played for time. 'I can't get all the money right now because the police have already been round to see me about Olga.' It was a classic Elizabeth lie. 'If I start taking that kind of money out of the bank they'd get real suspicious.'

'You gotta have *some* dough for us?' asked Moya.

'Sure,' agreed Elizabeth.

So a meeting was set up for the following day at the Blue Onion restaurant. Mrs Esquivel acted as the go-between because Moya and Elizabeth did not want to be seen meeting together in public. Moya had earlier warned Mrs Esquivel. 'I'll get real angry if she doesn't come up with the dough.'

Elizabeth offered the two drifters a cheque worth $200 and promised the rest of the money would follow 'very soon'. The cheque had actually been given to Elizabeth by her beloved son Frank to buy a typewriter. Little did he know his own money was being used to pay off the killers of his young, pregnant wife.

Naturally, Moya turned nasty and demanded cash. Another rendezvous was fixed up for a couple of hours later that day. This time Elizabeth handed Moya an envelope. When he opened it in his car a couple of minutes later it turned out to contain just $150. Over the next few days, Moya hounded Elizabeth for money but none appeared, except for a miserly $10 which she left for him in an envelope marked 'Dorothy' at the Blue Onion restaurant.

Meanwhile police enquiries prompted by Olga's disappearance had uncovered the full depth of anger that Elizabeth felt towards her daughter-in-law. When she was hauled in for questioning, she deflected attention by claiming she was being blackmailed by two Mexicans who'd threatened to kill her beloved son Frank. She even gave detectives descriptions of Moya and Baldonado – a curious move considering they both held the key to the actual crime that had been committed. The police then set up a phone-monitoring system to record any future calls from the supposed blackmailers. Elizabeth pulled the plug out of the recorder in her home to ensure she was not caught making her own incriminating statements.

On 4 December 1958, police picked up Moya and charged him with suspected blackmail. He was placed in an identity parade but Elizabeth failed to pick him out. Then the tormented Frank finally cracked and confronted his evil mother for the first time in his life. He accused her of covering up the truth. But she still refused to admit her role in Olga's disappearance. Meanwhile Moya was released and on his way out of the police station, he encountered Elizabeth and whispered to her, 'I think everythin' is goin' to be OK.'

Investigators then uncovered the truth about Elizabeth's involvement in the bogus attempt to annul Frank's marriage. Detectives also located Elizabeth's dotty old friend Mrs Emma Short, who suffered from the early signs of senile dementia. However, when the police called round at her home she poured out the entire story about the murder plot and how Olga was to be killed in Mexico. Mrs Short said she was terrified of Elizabeth Duncan and felt an undercurrent of violence every time the two women met. She told police she'd been too scared to report anything earlier, but now she knew it was time to speak up or be accused of conspiring with her friend in the murder of Olga.

Police obtained confirmation of Mrs Short's bizarre claims from the equally scared Mrs Esquivel. Baldonado was immediately hauled in for questioning, but refused to talk so he was jailed on a holding charge of failing to support his children. Moya was then re-arrested for violating his parole on an earlier conviction.

But there was still no sign of Olga's body and Elizabeth Duncan's lips remained sealed even though she was arrested and thrown in prison on a holding charge. In jail, she immediately began planning her escape and even offered bribes to other inmates to help her. Detectives knew they stood little chance of convicting anyone on the word of Mrs Short and Mrs Esquivel. They needed a confession from one of the main players or else they'd all walk free.

Eventually it was Baldonado who cracked. He knew that Elizabeth had conned both him and Moya and refused to let her get away with it. So he led them to Olga's battered remains – on condition that he didn't have to watch them dig her up. Shortly afterwards, Moya also confessed. With Mrs Short and Mrs Esquivel both granted immunity from prosecution, would Elizabeth finally confess? Not on your life: she carried on spinning her web of lies.

At her trial in March 1959, any suggestion that Elizabeth Duncan might be insane was thrown out by the court. A psychiatirst proclaimed that Elizabeth suffered from 'what is known in medicine as a personality trait disorder, more commonly called psychopathic personality ... But my findings are that she is not insane.' All three defendants were eventually found guilty of murder in the first degree. Each was sentenced to death.

Over the next three and a half years, a succession of appeals were made in a bid to stave off the executions. And the man leading the fight was none other than Elizabeth's beloved son Frank. Eventually he made a personal plea to a federal judge in San Francisco for yet another last-minute stay of execution, but this time his appeal fell on deaf ears. Finally Elizabeth Duncan, Luis Moya Jnr and Gus Baldonado headed for the gas chamber at San Quentin Prison on 8 August 1962.

Elizabeth Duncan, still an outwardly respectable-looking woman in late middle age, settled into the cold steel chair as if she was about to start a lengthy knitting session. She made herself comfortable before fixing her gaze on the two guards strapping down her arms.

'Where's Frank?' she asked sternly. No one reacted so she closed her eyes slowly and took her final four deep breaths. At 10.12am, Elizabeth Duncan was pronounced dead.

Three hours later Moya and Baldonado smiled pleasantly as they entered the same room. They sat in chairs marked A and B and continued their friendly banter even after a lever had been pulled to release the cyanide pellets into the vat of acid beneath their chairs.

As the poisonous fumes wafted upwards their moods finally changed. 'I can smell it,' said Moya. 'And it doesn't smell good.'

Ten minutes later both men were dead.

Chapter Five:

JIMMY MOODY
O.B.E

Combine the Kray Twins and the Richardsons with a sprinkling of guv'nor Lenny McLean, plus an IRA hitman thrown in for good measure and you start to get an idea of Jimmy Moody's underworld credentials.

And as they say in gangland Britain: 'He may be dead but his spirit lives on.' For Moody's career spanned more than four decades and included run-ins with Jack Spot, Billy Hill, 'Mad' Frankie Fraser, the Krays, the Richardsons and the Provos.

James Alfred Moody was number one enforcer for the Richardsons, did freelance 'work' for the Krays and became one of the most feared gangsters ever to emerge from the London underworld – all before he reached 30. And, just like the Krays, he worshipped his dear old mum.

Moody's first starring role came when he survived one of South London's most legendary club battles at a venue called Mr Smith's and the Witchdoctor's, a cabaret and gambling house in Catford in the early 1960s. A fight kicked off in the early hours when small-time hood Dickie Hart started waving a pieces around and shot another villain called Harry Rawlings. Hart was then plugged on the spot. All hell then broke lose and Jimmy Moody ended up carrying the wounded, including Eddie Richardson and Frankie Fraser, out of the club before disappearing in a cloud of smoke. Moody was later aquitted of any involvement in the shootings.

Some reckon the battle inside Mr Smith's was deliberately engineered by the Krays, who wanted to dismantle the Richardsons' powerbase. As James Morton says in his book *Gangland Britain*: 'This was an attempt by the Krays – with whom the Richardsons were, at the time, in serious disagreement over the rights to provide security for a blue-film racket in the West End – to dispose of their rivals once and for all.'

Jimmy Moody's reputation got another boost in 1967 when he was convicted of manslaughter over the death of a young merchant navy steward called William Day. Moody copped a six-stretch for that little number. In the clink, Moody became a committed body builder and on his release joined a notorious band of armed robbers known as the Chainsaw Gang which specialised in highjacking security vans in south London and the home counties.

Moody was a quiet, reserved sort of fellow who tended to stand back on the edge of a crowd and remain in the showdows keeping an eye on things. As such he was an important member of the Richardsons' inner circle. Moody was their official 'enforcer' – a godfather, feared and respected by the London underworld.

One time, Moody, dressed as a copper, jumped out of a motor in the Blackwall Tunnel and forced a security van to stop. To prevent anyone raising the alarm, he leaned into nearby cars and lobbed their keys into the gutter. In 1980, Moody was on the run from the law after yet another 'chainsaw gang' hijack when he visited a relative's flat in Brixton and was nicked for a series of blaggings involving a massive total of £930,000. He was then locked up in Brixton on remand.

In those days it was still possible for inmates awaiting trial to have food, wine and beer brought in by friends and relatives. One Sunday lunchtime Moody's brother Richard brought in hacksaw blades, drill bits and other tools. Within days Moody, his cellmate, IRA bomber Gerard Tuite, and Stan Thompson, a vet from the Parkhurst Prison riots of 1969 now banged up on an armed robbery charge, had begun cutting their way through the brickwork. On 16 December, 1980, they pushed out the loosened masonary of their cell, stepped onto a roof where a ladder had been left by workmen and were on their toes. Tuite and Moody vanished while Thompson was soon tracked down.

But Moody's story only took on legendary proportions after he went on the lam from Brixton Prison. Moody's cellmate Tuite told him countless tales of brutality and torture inflicted by the British across the water. Moody even looked a touch Irish with his heavy build, thick black eyebrows and bulldog neck. Once across the water in Ireland, Moody's murderous skills were soon put to good use by the Provos. He became their secret deadly assassin – a man who struck so much fear into Northern Ireland's security services that at one stage in the mid-1980s the Thatcher Government assigned a three-man hit-team of crack SAS men to finish him off.

It was then Moody coined the most chilling gangster-fuelled phrase of all time when he began referring to his victims as having been awarded an O.B.E. (One Behind the Ear). It went on to become the calling card used by many Belfast killers over the following 15 years. Moody himself fine-tuned his skills as a hitman to become the number one hired killer on both sides of the water. He was even renowned for professionally disposing of his victims' bodies if that was part of the contract or making sure that death occured in a public place as a 'message' to others.

But there was undoubtedly a human, caring side to this cold-blooded killer. While on the run in Ireland, Moody desperately missed his wife Val and their two kids back in Dulwich, South London. The cozzers almost nicked him in London when he flew in for a reunion with his son. He only got away when he was tipped off about a police and scarpered minutes before a posse of the local Old Bill swooped.

And in the middle of all this, Moody even deliberately fed informers, including the British security services, with inaccurate information which enabled him to survive on the run for more years than anyone else – with the exception of Ronnie Biggs.

By the late 1980s, Moody knew full well that he was in danger of over-staying his welcome on the Emerald Isle. The lure of London and all his old mates persuaded Moody to return to the smoke. He was convinced his reputation as a hired killer would keep him one step ahead of trouble – and the law.

But the 'smoke' he returned to was a very different place from the one he'd left ten years earlier. Huge drug deals – usually involving Ecstasy and cocaine – had taken over from armed robbery as a way of financing the lavish lifestyles of many criminals. The stakes were higher and so were the profits. Even a hardened soul like Jimmy Moody was disturbed by what he saw. He warned his own children to steer clear of drugs. But then he was renowned as a man who would not even tolerate other people smoking in his company.

However, Moody still had to earn a crust and, in the middle of all this, it's rumoured he knocked off one or two of the most notorious faces in London. They'd got up the noses of their drug baron mates big time. Moody knew that his reputation as a real hardman had to be maintained in the face of all these multi-millionaire drug barons. In 1990, the cozzers named him as the chief suspect in the 'plugging' of a member of one notorious south London criminal family. Moody never denied his involvement. However, he told one oldtime gangster that he knew he never should have taken the job because that family had never done him harm in the past and now they were after his blood.

'Jimmy knew he'd made a mistake and that he might end up paying the ultimate price for topping that geezer,' explained the south east London villain.

Moody even told his wife Val he wanted to turn over a new leaf and retire from gangsterdom before it was too late. He always defended himself in public by insisting he never once killed an innocent person. 'Each and every one of them deserved what they got; they were toerags,' he told one old mate.

Moody got himself work in a pub in the East End. He had a new name, a new job and life seemed reasonably sweet. Even though he prided himself on keeping a low profile, Moody believed he was better off on familiar territory. As another old timer later explained: 'You got more chance of surviving on home territory. There's always someone to let you know the cozzers are sniffing around or a face from another manor is on your tale. It makes total sense.'

But by the early 1990s Jimmy Moody's list of enemies read like a Who's Who of criminal faces from across both sides of the water. There was also the police, the RUC and the British security services. It was only a matter of time before someone's barrel pointed in his direction.

Moody was now known as 'Mick the Irishman' and he was finally awarded his own O.B.E. on the night of 1 June 1993, while drinking at the bar of the Royal Hotel, in Hackney. Three bullets to the head and one to the back from a hitman special – ironically, a .38 revolver just like Moody's favourite weapon of choice.

The fellow who shot Moody was in his early 40s, wearing a leather bomber jacket. The shooter had even first ordered his own pint of Foster's lager and put two coins down on the bar to pay for it. Then he turned towards Moody and carried on blasting away as he slumped to the floor. The killer fled in a stolen Ford Fiesta that was parked up just outside the pub.

At the time of his demise, Jimmy Moody had been living in Wadeson Street, a back alley off Mare Street, in Hackney. Some reckoned that Moody was topped because he was banging someone's missus. Others pointed the finger at a power-struggle between two south London gangs. Then there was the IRA and the British security services.

Frankie Fraser in his book *Mad Frank* has another take on Jimmy Moody's demise: 'It now turns out that Jimmy Moody was working in a pub at the back of Walworth. He'd been in the area for ten years. He wasn't an out-and-out nightclubber so he could have been there and very, very few people would know who he was. He's done quite a bit of bird and now he took it as a personal thing to keep out. It was a personal challenge for him. He could be stubborn and obstinate, a good man but a loner. He'd be content to do his work and watch the telly knowing that every day was a winner. That's how he would look at it.'

The mother of the one of Moody's most recent victims said: 'I'm glad Moody's dead. My family is overjoyed. He got it the way he gave it out. I'm glad he didn't die straight away. That man was evil and I hope he rots in hell.'

Jimmy Moody was a unique modern day figure whose activities have had an ominous knock-on effect on Britain's criminal underworld to this day. He perfectly encapsulated the archtypical London criminal. But he'd incurred the wrath of numerous gangsters and, as we now know, even members of the Provisional IRA. So it was no surprise that a price was put on his head.

Jimmy Moody pulled no punches. His life revolved around violence, black humour, the bizarre and the unemotional. But he was prepared to go beyond those traditional boundaries in order to make his name in the underworld. If you live by the sword you will eventually die by it...

Chapter Six:

BARRY THE BASTARD

Every morning, private eye Barry Trigwell's colleague John Waight picked him up from his home in Sutton Coldfield, near Birmingham, because Trigwell was banned from driving. When Waight arrived on Wednesday, 8 February 1995 and spotted the kitten mewing on the doorstep, he knew something was wrong. He rang the doorbell. No answer. He dialled Trigwell on his mobile phone. Still no answer.

Waight looked up and down the quiet cul-de-sac of Fowey Close. It was deserted. Then he peered through the lounge window of the modest, three-bedroomed red-brick house and saw bloodstains on the carpet. He called the police.

Inside the house, officers found a trail of blood stretching from the lounge to the bathroom. Trigwell's battered body, clad only in a pair of trousers, was floating in the half-filled bath. He'd been repeatedly beaten with a blunt object and had suffered severe fractures to his skull, face and body. His blood-soaked shirt was found discarded in the bathroom. It later emerged that the gun used by his attackers had failed to go off so they'd used a poker to batter Trigwell to death.

Police quickly established from neighbours that, at 7pm the previous evening, Barry Trigwell had arrived home after a meal alone at his local Indian restaurant. It looked as if he'd only been back in the house for a few minutes when there was a knock at the door.

Barry Trigwell's body was just being removed from the house by coroners' officials when his wife, Anne, rang the couple's home from South Africa, where she was on a business trip. An officer attending the scene broke the news to her and she said she'd fly home immediately.

Detectives initially set out to trace Trigwell's client list in the search for clues. He'd first started work as a freelance detective in 1974. Trigwell was so well known he relied on specialist clients and did not even bother listing himself in the professional directories. He also wasn't a member of the Association of British Investigators, which has a strict code of practice.

There were rumours that Trigwell had been heavily involved in investigating money launderers, a type of crime that could be particularly dangerous when the money was coming from the proceeds of drugs. There were other stories about how he'd been shadowed by Special Branch following a mysterious death in a case he was investigating.

Detectives soon found that assembling a list of suspects wasn't difficult. As John Clarke, who worked as an investigator with Trigwell at Nationwide Investigations in Birmingham, explained: 'He was known as "Barry the Bastard" by people he crossed. He really enjoyed snatching children back from abroad after one of the parents had skipped the country. He seemed to live for the adrenaline rushes.'

Colleagues described Trigwell as a short, stocky character who looked more like a Chicago gangster than a Brummie gumshoe. As John Clarke added, 'He'd been caught up in some heavy stuff. Barry charged a lot of money but he was really good at his job. When some of us may have taken a step back for fear of the consequences, Barry would just go for it. Barry made many enemies in his life.' But since his latest marriage, Trigwell had turned his back on the more dangerous aspects of his chosen profession and had even been spending increasing amounts of time in his new wife's home country.

Detectives then discovered from Trigwell's sister that in the weeks before his death, Trigwell had taken several mysterious calls at home from a South African man who wanted to meet him on a 'business matter'. Trigwell was immediately suspicious because he *never* gave his home number to clients and the caller was evasive when he asked the man how he'd obtained it.

Trigwell had even dialled the 1471 BT callback service, taken the number of the caller and given it to his sister Julie Armener, who lived in Eastbourne, Sussex, telling her to hand it to police if anything happened to him. Barry feared that someone was playing games with him. The number turned out to be a hotel where staff immediately remembered two South African men staying around the time the calls were made. They'd been back to stay at the hotel the week of Trigwell's death.

Back in Fowey Close, neighbours told police that a white

Fiat Punto had been parked outside the Trigwells' house shortly before the killing. It was traced to a hire company in London used by the same two South Africans who'd been staying at the hotel.

Police believed that Trigwell's two killers had not yet left the UK. They were traced to a hotel near Heathrow Airport but by the time detectives got to the scene the two men had caught a flight to Vienna and then South Africa, which did not have an extradition treaty with the UK.

Investigators then turned their attention towards Anne Trigwell. Friends said that she was well suited to her new husband, since they were both arrogant and shared a taste for gambling, sex and the high life. On the surface, Anne seemed rich and successful, having bought a $400,000 house with a swimming pool outside Johannesburg.

Trigwell, who had a 14-year-old daughter from an earlier marriage, and Anne Brooks had first met when she hired him to protect her. All he was told was that his client was involved in a large cash transaction and needed him to ensure it went without any problems. The minute Trigwell met his slim, good-looking client in her expensive heels he was smitten, and he soon began sending flowers to the Porsche-driving widow every week. Then she'd fly over to visit him at his rented house in the Midlands. Proud Barry even took her to see his hotelier father Leonard and mother Mary at their home in Eastbourne.

'She started calling us Mum and Dad straight away,' Mary Trigwell later recalled. 'She would ask us for a hug and put her arms around us but there was no real feeling.'

Barry Trigwell was soon sending thousands of pounds each month to pay Anne's mortgage on her South African mansion and to fund a host of ill-conceived business ideas. 'At first Anne turned down Barry's marriage proposals,' his mother Mary later recalled. 'Still he kept supporting her and went to South Africa to re-mortgage her house in his name. Then on a visit to us they announced they were to marry.'

The couple's wedding was held at Birmingham Register Office in 1994. Barry Trigwell was earning in excess of £3,000 a week by this stage and must have seemed a good catch to Anne. She even rented out her South African home to a local businessman and the newlyweds set up home together in Sutton Coldfield.

Then, in January 1995, police in South Africa were tipped off about a murder plot in which the businessman was overheard by his attractive wife talking about a planned hit. The businessman was said to have offered another South African £8,750 to kill someone. He in turn was alleged to have been offered more than £175,000 to arrange the killing. His wife agreed to help South African police organise a sting operation to arrest him but it failed and she disappeared in fear of her life. Detectives still had no idea who was the intended target.

In fact, the businessman had hired those same two men who'd turned up in the Midlands around the time of Barry Trigwell's murder. On 14 January 1995, they'd also made a reconnaissance trip to the UK. During that five-day visit they'd called Barry Trigwell's home requesting a business meeting. The pair then returned to the UK early in February to fulfil the contract. Between those two visits,

Trigwell's wife had left a sealed envelope containing £300 in 'expenses money' and a Yale front door key at the hotel where they stayed.

The envelope proved to be 42-year-old Anne Trigwell's downfall. Hotel staff, suspecting that it contained drugs, opened it, inspected the contents, re-sealed it and then, having no reason not to, duly passed it on to the two South Africans.

It was only after hearing about Trigwell's murder and the fact he had a dark-haired South African wife that the hotel recalled the similar woman with a 'funny' accent. That sparked the police investigation into Mrs Trigwell. Ten days after Barry Trigwell's slaying, his wife Anne was charged with plotting to kill him. She was remanded in custody by magistrates in Sutton Coldfield, West Midlands.

But being incarcerated wasn't going to stop temptress Anne Trigwell. Within a couple of months of her arrest, she'd begun a clandestine relationship with a prison officer called John Burns who was separated from his wife and young daughter. For the first six weeks of her incarceration they'd been the model of an upstanding warder–prisoner relationship. He'd lock her up in her second floor cell at Risely Prison, near Warrington. She would obey his barked orders.

Then fate intervened. On the way back from a magistrates' hearing in June 1995, Burns found himself sitting in the prison van next to Trigwell. The van braked sharply and their lives were never the same again. Burns later explained: 'We literally fell into each other's arms. We made eye contact and I felt immediate and immense attraction as I looked into her brown eyes. I can't explain it. It was just there.'

Their first proper embrace occurred when Burns was escorting Trigwell late at night along a deserted corridor in Risley's Windsor House section. They stopped and kissed passionately. As three-times-married Trigwell pulled him closer into the embrace she told him: 'I've been waiting for this moment for so long.'

Burns was so smitten that he couldn't get Anne Trigwell out of his mind. Later, many would ask how he could throw away a 17-year career for a woman whose speciality was to kiss and kill the men in her life. But Burns just didn't look at it that way. He explained: 'From the moment when I weakened and kissed her, I knew my career in the prison service was as good as over.'

Soon they were exchanging love notes and speaking of travelling to Trigwell's beloved South Africa, to which she dreamed of returning. Burns slipped scribbled messages under her cell door; she would discreetly hand him notes as he unlocked her cell each morning. Love trysts were held in the prison library. 'It was the only place where we could be together,' Burns later recalled. 'It was difficult, but somehow we were never caught. We wanted each other so much.'

One note written by Anne Trigwell read: 'Darling John. How it hurts to see you go, but this will soon end. Then we will be together forever. Please know one thing; that I love you, oh so very much it really hurts. You really are the one I trust and will give my love, life and heart to!' Another read: 'Your hands caress my every curve, sending sensations through every nerve.' They were almost word for word the same as the letters she'd written to Barry Trigwell.

Burns explains: 'I read and re-read these letters nearly

every day. Often I'd stand in her cell and we would just hold each other. I think I needed her as much as she needed me.'

In the middle of all this, Burns went to the prison authorities after Anne Trigwell offered him £50,000 to help her escape from jail. The authorities were never told that the two were having a relationship. It was only in November 1995 that love letters between Trigwell and Burns were found by other staff in her cell. Burns was re-interviewed by police and confirmed the relationship but was released because he hadn't broken any laws. He was suspended on full pay. Worried prison officials then transferred Trigwell to the maximum-security wing at Durham Jail, where other inmates have included IRA terrorists, Rose West and Myra Hindley.

However, Trigwell continued writing to Burns, whose letters back to Trigwell were never intercepted by the prison screening system. Burns claimed he had no regrets. 'Working in a prison can be a soul-destroying job,' he said. 'People don't understand that. That's why people can't understand that meeting Anne has been a good thing for me.'

Meanwhile, police in South Africa pulled in the nightclub boss plus the two other South Africans for questioning. They were eventually bailed by a court because there was no concrete evidence linking them to Barry Trigwell's murder.

Then, in June 1996, British detectives once again tracked down the businessman's estranged wife and she agreed to help investigators. Fearing for her life, she'd been travelling Europe and even had a bodyguard at her hideout in Italy. Police believed a hitman had been contracted to track her down and kill her. As one investigator explained: 'She undoubtedly put herself at enormous risk. There is no doubt in my mind that threats were made against her by the criminal underworld.'

The following month, Anne Trigwell's trial got under way at Birmingham Crown Court. She emphatically denied the murder. The jury heard that she had a secret boyfriend in South Africa and stood to gain £380,000 from bonds and insurance policies on the death of her husband. In other words, he was worth a lot more dead to her than alive. Timothy Raggatt QC, for the prosecution, said, 'He [Trigwell] was killed to order as a result of a plan. His death had been paid for. It was cold-blooded and very, very carefully planned.' Mr Raggatt told the court that the Trigwells' marriage was 'a disaster from the start'. He also said that if Mrs Trigwell had hired the hitmen 'she is as guilty of his murder as if she had beaten him to death herself'.

The court then heard that the three men involved with the killing were still at large in South Africa and Anne Trigwell had an alibi of 'enormous proportions' as she was 6,000 miles away at the time of her husband's death.

The court was told that in December 1994, Anne Trigwell flew to South Africa to spend Christmas with her family and that was when she asked the nightclub boss if he'd organise a hit on her husband. He then hired the two assassins. Prime prosecution witness, the businessman's estranged wife, told the court she'd overheard the contract being discussed. She remained in hiding because of real fears for her personal safety.

Further evidence in court came from Barry Trigwell's sister

Julie Armener who told how, at a dinner party two months before Trigwell's murder, her brother had become suspicious that his wife was having an affair and suggested he might accompany her on her next visit to South Africa. She leaned across the table and grabbed him by the jumper and said, 'If you come to South Africa I will have you shot and I know at least two people who will do it.'

Anne Trigwell then admitted in court that on the night before Barry Trigwell's murder she'd even paid for a celebration dinner with her lover, a 43-year-old game hunter called Jan Burger, and that they'd spent that night together. Prosecutors claimed she'd only flown back to Britain to pick up the death certificate so that she could cash in the insurance policies. But her sister-in-law had already been to the police and told them about those threats made by Anne as well as the phone number of the hotel traced by Barry Trigwell.

Anne Trigwell – dressed in a dark-blue jacket and tartan trousers – showed no emotion when the jury returned their guilty verdict. Mr Justice Nelson said that she'd been found guilty of conspiring in and planning the 'cold, calculated and chilling murder from afar and had actively ensured that the killers were able to perform their gruesome and vicious task'.

Her mother, Pat Bullock, and the victim's mother, Mary, who was sitting four rows in front of her, both burst into tears when the jury returned their verdict. Trigwell's prison officer lover John Burns sat throughout her trial with her relatives in the public gallery. Trigwell frequently glanced at Burns and he – along with her mother, teenage daughter Nicollette and sister Susan – were allowed a few minutes with her in the court cells before she was taken off to prison at the end of her case.

John Burns was shattered by the guilty verdict against Anne Trigwell and her subsequent life sentence. He resigned from the prison service 24 hours afterwards. 'Now both our lives are in a mess,' he admitted after the case. 'But I don't really regret sacrificing my career for her. I will wait as long as it takes. With luck she will be out in 12 years and we will both begin our new life in South Africa. We talked all the time of living there, going on safari and sleeping under the stars.'

Outside the court, Barry Trigwell's father Leonard described his daughter-in-law as 'an evil woman'. Mr Trigwell told reporters he felt as if he and his wife Mary had witnessed 'something out of James Bond'. Mr Trigwell continued, 'I thank the police for bringing this evil woman to justice. She coldly manipulated this crime. No one could ever have suspected that she would have done this. I am convinced that she only married our son to get hold of his money. She was clever and devious and lied to try to cover her tracks. I hope she rots in prison.'

It then emerged that Anne Trigwell's stepson by a previous marriage, Craig Paton, had died of head wounds caused by a gun registered in her name. Mr Paton had earlier inherited a substantial sum of money yet his death was deemed to be suicide. His father also died around the same time and senior investigating officer Detective Superintendent Kenneth Evans said he was planning to look more closely into the circumstances surrounding the death.

After the case, Anne Trigwell's second husband, Ray

Brooks, 58, said he was convinced Craig would not have committed suicide. He also said he believed that if he'd been a richer man he would also be dead today. 'She was vivacious, she knew she could get men and money, and went after it.'

Chapter Seven:

THE ULTIMATE HITMAN

No book about hitmen would be complete without a chapter on the most infamous, notorious and deadly triggerman of all – Carlos the Jackal. For more than 20 years he outwitted the forces of international intelligence. He was the world's most ruthless killer and kept his pursuers at bay thanks to the help of unscrupulous governments and by constantly changing his appearance.

Carlos was a master of disguise, altering his weight, hair and even his eye colouring. Travelling under a series of names ranging from Ahmed Adil Fawaz to Hector Dupont, and from Adolf Bernal to Flik Ramirez. He even employed doubles to lay a trail of confusion for his hunters. By the time he was finally apprehended in August 1994, Carlos the Jackal was held responsible for 83 murders across the globe.

Born Illich Ramirez Sanchez in Caracas, Venezuela, in

October 1949, Carlos was the son of a millionaire doctor of law who was a Stalinist left-winger. He gave his three sons the three names of Lenin – Illich, Vladimir and Lenin. Each of the brothers were given the best possible education. Illich's heroes were Che Guevara and Fidel Castro and he eventually learned to speak seven different languages fluently.

Illich travelled extensively from an early age and in 1966 lived for several months in central London, first in the King's Road and then in Wimpole Street, with his mother and brother Vladimir, before being sent by his father to the Patrice Lumumba Friendship University in Moscow: the world's most notorious finishing school for terrorists.

Officially, Illich was expelled in 1970 for 'riotous and dilettante behaviour', although many believe this may have been a line fed by the university in order to confuse the West about Illich's progress. In 1972, he enrolled at the London School of Economics.

However, within months, Illich joined the most feared terrorist group at that time, the Popular Front for the Liberation of Palestine, which eventually established close links to the Japanese Red Army and the Baader-Meinhof Group in Germany, who later provided Illich with a round-the-clock bodyguard. Other 'incorporated' groups included the Organisation for the Armed Arab Struggle and the Turkish Popular Liberation Front.

Illich used his superb expertise with firearms in order to convince these terrorist groups he could became their own one-man secret weapon. Soon Illich was boasting that his favourite method of killing was a bullet between the eyes. Illich clearly had a thorough indifference to human life, not to mention a talent for manipulating pretty young women. But more of that later.

One of Illich's earliest high-profile killings occurred in Paris in the summer of 1975, when he cold-bloodedly shot dead two French intelligence agents who'd gone to his Paris flat after a tip-off from Mossad, the Israeli intelligence service. Illich also gunned down the police informer who'd betrayed him and left a message declaring war on 'Zionist and imperialist targets in all parts of the world'.

Five days later in London, Illich had his closest shave with authorities. Three glasses of Bacardi and Coke were found half-empty when Scotland Yard detectives arrived in the smoke-filled downstairs bar of Angelo's Club in Bayswater. The man known to bar staff as a Peruvian economist called Carlos, and two pretty South American women who regularly accompanied him, had all vanished minutes before the detectives' arrival.

Scotland Yard swooped simultaneously on a network of west London flats used by the man known as Carlos – all rented by women on his behalf. Investigators uncovered a huge cache of arms, hand grenades and explosives. They also found a hit list of 500 Jewish businessmen and personalities in Britain, including politician Sir Keith Joseph, playwright John Osborne and violinist Sir Yehudi Menuhin.

But the man then known as Carlos Martinez had vanished off the face of the earth. Carlos the Jackal actually got his nickname from the fictional assassin sent to kill President de Gaulle in Frederick Forsyth's novel *The Day of the Jackal* – a copy of which was found in Carlos' Bayswater flat. Even by 1975 his file – held by British, French and German police –

was extensive. It included links to the massacre of 11 Israeli athletes at the Munich Olympics in 1972.

Carlos was also suspected of involvement in the wounding of British millionaire Edward Seiff – of the Marks and Spencer family – the following year. Then there was the seizing of the French Embassy in the Hague in 1974, the bombing of an Israeli bank in London the same year and a grenade attack on a crowded Paris café. Carlos was also sought in connection with a bazooka attack on an El Al Boeing at Paris's Orly Airport in January 1975. Carlos had a reputation for only carrying out spectaclar attacks and prided himself on his meticulous planning and uncanny ability to slip through any security net.

In December 1975, with security services throughout Europe hunting for him, Carlos managed to pull off his most spectacular coup when he masterminded an attack on the headquarters of Opec – the organisation of oil-producing states – in Vienna. Three people, including an Austrian policeman, were killed as his guerrillas took control of the offices and kidnapped 11 ministers.

Calling themselves 'the Arm of the Arab Revolution', the terrorists demanded a bus to take them and the hostages to a fuelled plane at the airport, a condition the Austrians eventually agreed to. The aircraft first flew to Algiers, where most of the hostages were freed, then on to the Libyan capital, Tripoli, before returning to Algiers where the guerrillas gave themselves up. They were freed within a couple of days.

One of the first real insights into Carlos's character came from a kidnapped oil minister he held at gunpoint. Asked what he was like, the minister explained: 'Quite charming, the kind of man that if he came home with your daughter you would be delighted.'

But behind that charm lay a ruthless, cold individual who thought nothing of throwing a grenade into a crowded restaurant or bar. At the beginning, his killings seemed rooted in idealism, but Carlos eventually became nothing more than a hired gun. Together with another legendary Middle East terrorist, Abu Nidal, he became known as the most efficient killing machine available to terrorist groups across the globe: the Ultimate Hitman.

Those who've encountered him over the past 35 years say he is an opportunist rather than a true fanatic. He is not a communist and is now even said to despise the Arabs. But his ability to seduce beautiful young women and convert them to the cause meant that at one stage in the mid-Seventies, more than a dozen different women were being interviewed by police in various parts of Europe about their links with him.

Not surprisingly, a lot of myths have grown around the so-called legend of Carlos the Jackal. He has been credited with numerous terrorist attacks he played no part in. But security services have definitely connected him to the 1976 hijacking of a French airliner to Entebbe, in Uganda, a drama which ended with an Israeli airborne commando raid to free the hostages.

Shortly after that operation, Carlos went to ground, living behind the Iron Curtain in both Hungary and East Germany as well as in the Middle East. There were unconfirmed sightings of him in London in 1978, and the following year he gave an interview to the Paris-based Arabic magazine, *al-*

Watan-al-Arabi, in which he challenged authorities to try and catch him.

Then Carlos's fingerprints were found on a letter sent to French Interior Minister Gaston Defferre in March 1982, threatening reprisals if his then girlfriend Magdalena Kopp and another activist, Bruno Breguet, were not released. On the day Kopp and Breguet were sentenced by a French court to five and four years respectively for arms and explosives offensives, a car bomb went off in Paris killing one person and wounding 60. Carlos did not claim responsibility for that bombing, although it carried all his hallmarks. However, he did admit to bombing a French cultural centre in West Berlin in August 1983.

A few months later, on New Year's Eve, fifty people were hurt when bombs exploded both in Marseille's main railway station and on board a high-speed train. Two letters claiming responsibility for the blasts on behalf of the Arab Armed Struggle were traced to Carlos, one through handwriting and the other through fingerprints, which had been on file since the killing of those two French security agents in Paris in 1975. A French court eventually sentenced him in his absence to life imprisonment for these killings.

But even before the collapse of communism, Carlos' terrorist paymasters were growing tired of his antics. His small, highly trained group of killers had taken to heavy drinking and hiring prostitutes, and one of their favourite party tricks was shooting up the ceilings of hotels.

Yet both the Soviet Union and Hungary still offered Carlos a safe haven. When Hungary's Communists fell, the new leaders found a 'thank you' note from Carlos to former president Janos Kadar.

Then Carlos turned for protection to the Middle East – to Baghdad (where he is said to be a personal friend of Saddam and to have carried out a number of attacks on his behalf) and then to Damascus where he lived for some time with his German terrorist lover Magdalena Kopp and their two children, after her release from a French jail.

Then, in 1991, with new alliances built up during the Gulf War, Carlos was told he had to leave Baghdad. He went to Libya but was turned away and then surfaced in Yemen. Security services throughout the world were shadowing his movements and he was running out of places to hide. When civil war broke out in Yemen, Carlos fled again, this time to Sudan, entering Khartoum on a false diplomatic passport. Within weeks he was being linked with the Iranian-backed Hezbollah movement, which was behind a number of bombings on Israeli targets in London at the time. They were rumours that Carlos had come out of self-imposed 'retirement' to plan some even more outrageous terrorist attacks. The world held its breath.

Then on Sunday, 14 August 1994, the luck and cunning that had helped Carlos evade capture for so long finally ran out. Carlos was hauled out of his rented Khartoum apartment and arrested by a joint taskforce of French and Sudanese agents. He was immediately flown overnight by armed guards to La Sante Prison in Paris.

The Sudanese happily helped the French because they believed Carlos had arrived in Khartoum to plan assaults on foreign targets in the country. Agents had him under surveillance even before the French requested his arrest.

Several other people were also arrested during the raid on Carlos's modest apartment.

Today, Carlos' home is a drab, grey 127-year-old prison, overlooking a tree-lined Parisian boulevard. Until Carlos's arrival, its most famous inmate had been former Nazi collaborator Paul Touvier, who was jailed for life in April 1994 over the 1944 execution of seven Jewish hostages. Carlos lives in complete isolation, so he does not mingle with any of the other 1,600 inmates.

Chapter Eight:

CLASSY

Sylvia Paterson was the ultimate gold-digger, who used charm and ruthless cunning to drag herself from humble beginnings right up the ladder to the richest lifestyle imaginable. Her eye for the main chance helped transform her from a scruffy council house kid into a jet-setter with two planes, two Rolls-Royces, a Mercedes and two Range Rovers. Flamboyant Sylvia drove each car with her own £20,000 personalised number plate: CLA55Y.

Yet just months after she was born in Kent more than 50 years ago, her mother walked out on the family. Sylvia then spent a lot of time in a children's home because her father couldn't cope with her and her three sisters. Later she was looked after by three spinster aunts but didn't find any real happiness until she married a soldier sweetheart called David Bardsley. The couple had a daughter, Julie, and a son, Tyrell. And Sylvia became a highly respected nurse, working alongside top doctor Patrick Steptoe when he produced the world's first test-tube baby in 1978.

Then Sylvia got her first real taste of the good life when she landed a £200,000-a-year job as personal assistant to a Lebanese business tycoon. Soon she was jetting around the world and discovering a lifestyle she hadn't even known existed. Inevitably, her long absences from home put a lot of strain on her marriage and it eventually crumbled.

Sylvia openly admitted to friends she was more in love with those material gains than her husband. She even splashed out much of her high salary on privately educating Julie, now 33, at Cheltenham Ladies College and Tyrell, now 28, at Stowe. Sylvia then started dabbling in several businesses including a property speculation company in up-and-coming Cheshire. Then she met another property developer called John Holmes by chance when she called at his dry cleaning business as a customer following her divorce in 1981. The pair hit it off immediately and teamed up to form a property company called Paterson-Holmes acquiring properties in Hale, Cheshire, and Park Lane, London.

Sylvia impressed Holmes with her stories of jetting to New York on Concorde and he also greatly respected her business sense. 'She is extremely clever. One of the best negotiators I have ever met,' he later recalled. The pair talked about buying a nightclub called Yesterdays in Alderley Edge, which is near the Cheshire home of David and Victoria Beckham. They also planned to invest in a villa in France. Soon Sylvia was able to afford to buy her own £650,000 home in upmarket Wilmslow.

Then she met retired company boss Ken Paterson at a local pub. His first wife had died a year earlier and Sylvia instantly set her sights on becoming his wife and heiress. But Ken's son Paul and his wife Sarah almost immediately began to suspect Sylvia's motives. Soon their relationship with Sylvia descended into utter hatred and contempt. They began trading insults in a flurry of faxes. One message from Paul and his wife Sarah to Sylvia read: 'As soon as you cause Ken any measure of unhappiness, we will be there to comfort and support him. We will never go away.'

Soon elderly Ken was having to see his beloved grandchildren in secret behind Sylvia's back. His son Paul then hired a private detective to find out more about the woman he still believed was trying to get her hands on the family fortune.

Paul and his wife Sarah even refused to attend Ken Paterson's wedding to Sylvia the following year. And in another of their many faxes, Sylvia bizarrely claimed that her daughter-in-law had almost run her down when she was crossing a road in Wilmslow. In another fax, she called Paul and Sarah 'wicked' and accused them of waging a 'futile vendetta'.

But the last straw for Sylvia came when she discovered that her husband intended leaving his multi-million-pound fortune to his son Paul – not her. That was when Sylvia Paterson turned to her business partner John Holmes for advice. She told Holmes she wanted both her stepson and his wife to 'just disappear'.

To his friends and neighbours, John Holmes was a tireless

charity champion who'd once splashed out £3,600 for a painting by Prince Charles at a fundraising auction. But behind the benevolent façade lurked a vicious, cold-hearted man addicted to cocaine and spanking call girls. For while Holmes' photo regularly appeared in high-society magazines rubbing shoulders with the rich and famous at champagne charity functions, he was so proud of his criminal associates he kept a photo of the Kray twins in his bathroom.

And none of Holmes' influential pals from the wealthy 'Cheshire set' realised he'd also served time in jail for molesting a 16-year-old waitress. In August 1998, Holmes had been given a two-month jail sentence for groping the waitress during a party at a bistro in Knutsford. The court had heard how Holmes and another man tried to kiss the teenager and fondle her breasts. He'd even been placed on the sex offenders list. As one of Holmes' work associates later explained: 'He was completely ruthless and amoral. No one crossed him or stood in his way. He was determined to get what he wanted when he wanted it. That usually meant money and women. He loved sex.'

Yet, ironically, John Holmes came from the other end of the social scale to Sylvia Peterson. He was born at St Mary's Hospital, Manchester, in 1956, the youngest of the three children of the respectable Evelyn and John Holmes. His father was a Desert Rat war hero who served under Field Marshal Montgomery at El Alamein. Holmes attended Prince Charles's school, Gordonstoun, and left with two A-levels and five O-levels. He set out to make his fortune through a plant hire company, taxi firm and property speculation. His sister Marie married former Manchester City and England player

Colin Bell. His other sister, Jackie, was happily married with three children.

Holmes eventually used funds from the sale of his father's vastly successful tyre business to Uniroyal to start Park Dry Cleaners in Hale, Cheshire. It was such an upmarket establishment that it once got a recommendation in the pages of *Vogue* magazine.

Holmes had married his wife Christine more than 20 years earlier. They had a daughter, Sophie, 17, who has a rare muscle disorder, and 11-year-old twins, Jon and Camilla. All three children went to expensive private schools. The family lived in a £1.2 million mansion in Hale, Cheshire. One of his neighbours was former soccer boss and England ace Bryan Robson. Holmes also owned a £500,000 art collection, which allegedly included works by David Hockney and Salvador Dali.

John Holmes boasted of a personal fortune of £2–3 million. He and his wife even splashed out £10,000 to decorate one of their children's bedrooms like the cover of an Elton John album. And Holmes still found time to have an affair with escort agency boss Audrey Clarke as well as sharing hookers with his friends and work associates and regularly picking up women in bars. Audrey Clarke's company Class Act provided Holmes with numerous women. She'd first met him when Holmes called her agency by phone saying he 'needed a woman'.

Audrey arrived at Holmes's mansion in the early hours of the morning to be greeted by a scene of complete decadence. Ladies' underwear was draped around the bedroom. On a table were chopped-up lines of cocaine. A brunette woman was slumped in a chair with a glass of champagne in one hand and a cigarette in the other. 'I knew straight away that Holmes was an unusual man,' Audrey later explained.

Holmes then waved his arm towards the rather confused-looking girl and asked Audrey if she could get rid of her. 'At first I didn't know what to do or say,' recalled Audrey. 'I was confused. I asked why he couldn't just call her a taxi, but he just shrugged and said she wouldn't leave. He looked so helpless that I decided to help him out. When I spoke to the girl I realised she was stoned out of her mind. But I'd agreed a fee of £300 with Holmes, and I thought, What the hell? I've had more unusual requests.'

Audrey dressed the unprotesting woman and put her in a cab. Holmes then mentioned there were still a few hours left of their 'deal' and pointed to the bedroom. Audrey later recalled, 'John was a gentle lover, he reminded me of a little schoolboy. I don't know what had been going on, but he kept telling me how grateful he was to me for getting rid of the girl.'

Afterwards Holmes and Audrey sat chatting in the lavishly furnished lounge of his luxurious home. 'I remember putting my feet up on a huge marble coffee table and thinking, So this is what life's all about in the Cheshire set.' Then Audrey cracked open a new bottle of Bollinger and poured them both a drink. It was only then that Holmes properly introduced himself. He boasted about his wealth and important connections, even pointing to a photo on the mantelpiece of himself with then Tory leader William Hague and his wife Ffion. He talked about his contributions to charity, but also hinted at many criminal connections.

The following day Holmes rang Audrey, said his wife was still away and asked to see her. 'He also asked me to bring along another girl for a business friend.' The foursome ate at a local restaurant before going back to Holmes' mansion. Holmes then left Audrey and her friend alone at the house while they went out to buy some cocaine. Audrey refused to take any drugs when they returned, but found herself intrigued by Holmes' lifestyle.

But as the relationship developed over the next few months, Audrey began to see her lover in a disturbing new light. 'I realised that he used people quite ruthlessly and didn't seem to care who he hurt,' she said. 'He treated his staff like slaves. Then he started to let me down. He was always late, but one night he went too far. Out of the blue, he asked me if he could whip me. I was appalled. I told him I wasn't into that sort of thing.'

Holmes even asked Audrey if she could provide him with a girl who might be willing. A few weeks later there was an incident in which one of Audrey's 'girls' locked herself in the bathroom of one of Holmes' apartments after being told three men in the flat were expecting to have sex with her. Audrey forgave Holmes for the incident after he apologised and said he'd been drunk. But then he upset her again by showing her a set of photos of a woman who'd been severely whipped.

But the last straw in their so-called relationship came when Holmes asked Audrey to a charity function. She turned up to find him sitting at a table with his wife. Holmes saw her and persuaded her to stay. A few days later, Holmes arranged to meet Audrey in a local pub. He said he was also meeting a man known as Banjo. Holmes was late, as usual, so Audrey introduced herself to Banjo who immediately hinted at a mysterious background in the Armed Forces. 'I met him several times over the next couple of months. I knew he was involved in some big business deal with John, but I never dreamed they could be plotting a double murder,' Audrey later recalled.

In fact, John Holmes had recruited his ex-cellmate Paul Thorlsog – a former travelling circus clown known as Banjo – as the hitman who would wipe Sylvia Paterson's stepson Paul and his wife Sarah off the face of the earth. Banjo later recalled, 'I was asked if I was going to be discreet and I said, "Yes – I am a professional." But I had no intention of carrying out any killing. My intention was, once I got some money in my pocket, I'd disappear. Sylvia offered me £20,000 per person. But she couldn't make up her mind how she wanted it to happen.'

It was eventually agreed that Banjo would murder Paul and Sarah as they celebrated their 14th wedding anniversary on 27 April 1999. As Banjo later explained: 'For Sylvia it was all a matter of diabolical greed. She wanted to get her hands on the money. For John it was all a game. He liked to act like God and didn't want to look stupid in front of his criminal friends. He always had to be the big man.' However, 12 days before the designated day of the hit, Banjo the clown panicked and went to the police.

Detectives immediately launched Operation Gatehouse and sent in an undercover cop, whom Banjo introduced to Holmes and Peterson as a soldier more willing and able to carry out the contract. Paterson and Holmes were secretly tape-recorded as they talked about the intended murder and their scheme was uncovered before the killings could take place. At one stage, Holmes even told the undercover cop he could easily get 'Ruud Gullits' – rhyming slang for bullets. And he referred to someone being sent to a 'warm place' – a grave.

The next day both Holmes and Paterson were arrested.

At their trial at Manchester Crown Court, circus clown Banjo donned his civvies – a dapper grey pinstripe suit, a flat-top haircut and handlebar moustache – to tell the jury how Holmes and Paterson tried to recruit him as a hitman. Banjo/Thorlsog told the court: 'I was just interested in making some money. Who wouldn't?' He said he discussed the double hit during a series of meetings with Holmes and Paterson. He even said she admitted she wanted her stepson and his wife dead so she could reclaim her stake in the family business.

In court, Sylvia Paterson claimed she hired Banjo the clown purely to spy on her husband, whom she suspected was having an affair with a married woman. She also revealed to the court the full extent of her appalling relationship with her stepson Paul and his wife Sarah. How they'd first met at the couple's house when Sylvia was going with Ken Paterson to a cocktail party in December 1993. Dressed in a camel-coloured frockcoat, Paterson turned towards the jury and said, 'I was probably there for 15 minutes. Paul had a discussion with his father and Sarah didn't say anything. I was trying to talk to their little boy but it was difficult because he was having his dinner. We then went straight out of the front door and I have never been back since.' Sylvia and her elderly husband, Ken, had started divorce proceedings just before the trial started but Ken loyally stood by his wife and was even called as a defence witness during the proceedings.

Manchester Crown Court then heard how John Holmes had stayed in close contact with escort agency boss Audrey and she'd even visited him in prison while he awaited trial. However, after giving evidence against him, Audrey received two death threats, which were taken so seriously that she was given round-the-clock police protection. 'All my feelings for him have now disappeared. But I really did love him despite everything,' Audrey later explained.

Sylvia Paterson's QC maintained throughout the trial that she was innocent. But Judge Sir Rhys Davies called Paterson the 'driving force' behind the plot. And he told John Holmes: 'You enjoyed a very comfortable lifestyle. There is no one but yourself to blame for its destruction.' Neither of the defendants showed any emotion when the jury came back with a guilty verdict for both of them. Holmes and Paterson were each jailed for nine years for plotting the hitman murder of her stepson and his wife.

After the trial, intended targets Paul and Sarah Paterson said, 'We are very relieved. We knew nothing of the plot to kill us until the police came to inform us. We would like to thank the police for their unstinting support and can now look forward to returning to a normal family life.'

Meanwhile Banjo the clown remains in protective custody amid claims that Holmes has put a £250,000 contract out on his life.

Chapter Nine:

SPANISH BEDLAM

Tenerife, in the Canary Islands, was a picturesque place full of sunshine and good humour – until British holidaymakers started turning up in droves more than 20 years ago. They bring much of the money to the island but they also bring much of the trouble.

Many reckon that the area round Playa de las Americas is fast on its way to displacing the Costa del Sol as Spain's pre-eminent 'Costa del Crime'. Almost 20,000 Brits live permanently in the south of Tenerife and a large number of them are criminals who have a strong grip on the island's underworld, controlling the flow of drugs into Tenerife and dominating the shady world of timeshare. It's said that if you cross any of the criminal element you're likely to get a visit from men with baseball bats. Or you just disappear.

So Mick O'Hara, Gary Holmes, Stanley Stewart and Jacqueline Ambler were not exactly fish out of water. Holmes and Stewart both had records back in Britain for violent offences. O'Hara had seven convictions for offences including robbery and assault. Thirty-three-year-old Jacqui Ambler, from Rossington, near Doncaster, also had a couple of convictions, although her father later disputed this claim.

She'd divorced the father of her son and arrived on Tenerife with her new partner, Mick O'Hara, from Wakefield, Yorks, in March 1995. Back in Britain, he'd run a coal delivery firm and she'd helped out with the paperwork. They bought a British-style pub called Stevie's Bar on an avenue planted with palm trees that ran between a shopping precinct and an apartment hotel at the resort of Los Cristianos. It was a bizarre, overdeveloped district filled with rapidly constructed buildings completely out of sync with many of the older style properties.

Jacqui Ambler's bar wasn't exactly an investment in the future. She and Mick had fallen into the classic trap of believing that the rest of their lives could be turned into a holiday on the sunshine island. She'd even hoped that her 6-foot, 15-stone lover's violent temper might change in a warmer climate.

But that dream soon turned into a nightmare when Jacqui discovered that 39-year-old Mick's temper had got worse. Soon, neighbours in Playa de las Americas noticed the bruises and scars on her face and upper body.

The beatings rapidly got so bad that Jacqui decided on some drastic action. She got talking to bar regular Gary Holmes, from Littlehampton, Sussex, and asked to meet him later in a neighbouring bar. That was when she told him she wanted Mick to be killed. Jacqui informed him that her young son, who was on holiday, would be returning to England the following Tuesday and that she believed Mick O'Hara would kill her the moment the boy left the island. She said that Mick, in front of the boy, had 'previously' told her she had two years left 'to live'; that she was 'of no more use to him'.

Holmes and Jacqui agreed a plan to carry out the killing later that same day when all the customers had left Stevie's Bar.

Holmes, 31, later claimed that Jacqui offered him £4,000 as a down payment and a further £50,000 to be handed over later in Britain.

On 5 September 1995, Jacqui Ambler went out the back of Stevie's Bar saying she had to put the rubbish out. Holmes' 31-year-old friend Stanley Stewart, from Stirlingshire, then lured Mick O'Hara into the lavatory of O'Hara's bar by pretending the sink was blocked. The idea was to beat him unconscious and then stab him to death, but then Stewart slipped as he set about his intended victim and managed to do no more than grab him by the neck.

Then Holmes botched the stabbing when the blade bent before he could plunge it into O'Hara's heart. So Holmes broke a bottle over his head. But not even that was enough to knock out O'Hara, who then broke free and locked himself in the lavatory.

The two burly doormen fled but were stopped outside by Jacqui Ambler, who allegedly persuaded them to go back inside and finish him off. Seconds later, Jacqui lured O'Hara out by pretending his attackers had fled. As he emerged he was hit several times over the head with a metal container –

a beer barrel or gas bottle – before Holmes set about trying to strangle him with his own medallion chain.

But still O'Hara refused to go quietly, so Holmes stuffed a bar towel into his mouth and even up his nostrils to try suffocating him instead. That eventually did the trick. But by the time Holmes and Stewart were finished, their victim and his bar were smothered with blood.

Just a few hours later, Holmes and Stewart were both arrested and confessed to the murder. But what Holmes didn't realise was that there would be no going back on that first statement. Spain's legal system reserves its stiffest penalties for those about whose guilt there is no dispute and it is as harsh on premeditation as it is lenient on those driven by some spontaneous, momentary, uncontrollable passion.

Jacqui Ambler frequently broke down in floods of tears during her trial at the Palace of Justice in Tenerife's capital, Santa Cruz. She always maintained her innocence, constantly denying that she had plotted the killing and promised to pay the two men to kill O'Hara. However, Holmes and Stewart both made detailed statements shortly after they were arrested in which they described the events that led up to the killing.

But when the trial started, 30 months after their arrest, they changed their stories and Holmes claimed that he alone was responsible for O'Hara's murder. He insisted he'd killed the bar owner in a vicious fight over a drugs debt. Holmes said he'd made up the story about Jacqui Ambler hiring him and Stewart because he thought she had told police about his drugs trafficking.

Neither the court or the police made any attempt to check this new version and the question of drugs was not even mentioned throughout the trial. 'It has been shown that there was something more than a mere relation of acquaintanceship between Gary and Jacqueline,' remarked Judge Juan Manuel Fernandez del Toro Alonso.

But the big question was, when did their affair begin? If it was after the murder then it is not relevant, but if they were lovers before the killing, it would put a whole new light on the case. And the defendants' legal counsels were not permitted to challenge the prosecution's evidence in cross-examination.

One witness who didn't show up at the trial, a waiter called Clemente Alvarez Lopez, originally told police he'd seen Holmes in the bar with a Scotsman and a woman he did not recognise. Shown photos of Ambler by the police, he was unable to identify her as the woman, yet subsequently he picked her out twice in identity parades.

Another key witness was the owner of the bar next door to Stevie's Bar. Francisco Pacheco told police he'd seen two men talking to Ambler outside the bar at 4am, after the murder. He claimed to have seen the men earlier that evening. Yet he failed to identify either Holmes or Stewart in identity parades.

At one stage during the trial, Holmes even leapt to his feet and shouted at the Spanish judges: 'These people are innocent. I have put my friend and this woman behind bars for nearly three years already. You can do what you like to me but please let them go.' Stewart told the court he'd gone along with Holmes' claims because he was scared of him and 'of the men he worked for'.

Holmes told the court that Stewart's only involvement had been to try and break up the fight between himself and O'Hara. But the judges rejected the new versions and decided the original statements made to police and, under oath, to an investigating judge told what really happened.

In May 1998, Holmes and Stewart – both bouncers at another bar in Playa de las Americas – began what are thought to be the biggest sentences handed out to British subjects in Spain since the end of Franco's dictatorship: 29 years, just one year short of the maximum allowable under Spanish law. Jacqui Ambler's was given 27 years, 8 months and a day.

Back home in Rossington, Jacqui's father John, 61, said, 'There was no evidence against my daughter. Those first statements were made under duress. Twenty-seven years – I can't believe it. I never thought of anything but a "not guilty" verdict. We expected her to be freed and hadn't made plans for this. We can't understand how she could have been convicted. None of the prosecution's seven witnesses turned up and it just doesn't seem real.'

It is not clear how long the three defendants expect to remain behind bars. They had been held in the island's prison since their arrests almost immediately after the killing. In another case in the early Nineties, a Briton living on the Costa del Sol was jailed for 25 years for the murder of his wife but released after five. Meanwhile others have had to serve at least two-thirds of their sentence, meaning Ambler, Holmes and Stewart could end up serving at least 20 years each.

Shortly after the case, O'Hara's mother Doreen Emerson was astonished to receive a £2,500 bill by the court which had jailed her son's killers. Spanish law officers said the bill was for 'court work' connected to the case.

Doreen said, 'I have lost a son who meant the world to me and have had nothing but expense. The court demand is outrageous.'

The court bill came following disclosures about how Holmes and Ambler had been allowed sex sessions in their Tenerife jail for good behaviour.

Chapter Ten:

TWISTED FURY

Richardson, Texas. A quiet, middle-class suburb of Dallas. It is the early hours of the morning of 4 October 1983. Inside the bedroom of a house on Loganwood Drive lies a critically wounded young woman. She is naked, her wrists are tied to the bed and she is face down with two bullet wounds in the back of her head. Yet somehow she's still alive.

Just then, her four-year-old son walks into the bedroom. He looks down at his mother and tries to 'wake her up'. The child then rushes to the phone and calls his father: 'Momma is sick. I can't wake her up.' The father immediately calls the emergency services before rushing over to the house. Within minutes, the wailing sirens and blue-and-red lights of the emergency services flash in the distance as police units and paramedics swamp the area.

The size of the entry wounds to her head show that she's been shot with a small-calibre gun. Bloodstains cover the sheets, and a pillow punctured by two bullet-holes lies on the bedroom floor. Tissue paper is also spread across the floor. Rope is tied from her wrists to three of the bedposts. Another piece of rope lies on the carpet at the foot of the bed, next to a puddle of vomit. The brunette victim is unshackled by paramedics and rushed to a nearby hospital.

Outside, the victim's four-year-old son is crying hysterically in the garden as he's comforted by his father, who tells the police that the gunned-down woman is his 33-year-old wife, Rozanne Gailiunas, a registered nurse.

The boy's father told officers from nearby Richardson that he'd been estranged from the child's mother for the past few weeks. Investigators then immediately began knocking on houses in Loganwood Drive for possible witnesses. Not long afterwards, another man walked into the victim's front yard asking what had happened. Richard Finley explained he was a friend of Rozanne Gailiunas and said he'd last spoken to her by phone earlier the previous morning.

There were no signs of a forced entry to the house nor anything to indicate there'd been a burglary. Apart from on the bed, there were not even any signs of a struggle. Had the victim known her attacker and let him in the house? Or was she the victim of a random assailant who persuaded her to let him or her in?

Rozanne's young son told police that he and his mother had eaten at a fast food restaurant the previous lunchtime before she took him to a local ice rink. When they returned home later that day, Rozanne told her son to take a nap. When he woke up – probably because of the sound of the shots – he went to the living room to watch a film on the VHS machine but was unable to start it. The toddler then went to his mother's bedroom for help, found her tied to the bed and phoned his father.

Over at the Dallas hospital, Rozanne Gailiunas underwent life-saving surgery. Doctors warned detectives she might not live through the night and she died a few hours later without ever recovering consciousness. Police then began the painstaking process of piecing together Rozanne's life story.

Rozanne had met and married her doctor husband in their native state of Massachusetts before moving to Texas in 1972, when he took a job on the faculty of a Dallas medical school. She worked as a nurse in a local hospital and their son was born in 1979. Rozanne quit her nursing job to take better care of the boy. Plans were discussed to construct a brand new $500,000 home in an exclusive Dallas suburb. And by the beginning of 1983 the building was starting to take shape.

The couple's marriage started crumbling when Rozanne announced she 'wanted some space' to sort her life out and even proposed a return to nursing. In fact, she'd begun a passionate romance with a handsome building contractor who was working on their new home. Richard Finley was separated from his wife at the time and was the man who mysteriously arrived at the crime scene on the night of Rozanne's murder.

Investigators quickly checked out the alibis of Finley and the victim's husband. Both were able to account for their movements. Perhaps it was a random crime after all? At that time, serial killers were getting vast press coverage and the finger of suspicion was pointing in the direction of such a psychopath. Maybe he'd killed before?

Detectives contacted the FBI who submitted all the details of the Gailiunas killing to the VICAP – Violent Criminal Apprehension Program – specifically set up to track down such random acts by making computerised comparisons to other similar crimes across the United States. But there were no matches.

The police investigation into the slaying of Rozanne Gailiunas was eventually wound down as detectives ran out of leads. It was not until three years later – on the afternoon of 14 June 1986 – that an incident occurred which immediately re-ignited the inquiry.

Rozanne's lover Richard Finley reported to police that he'd been shot at while driving to his ranch with a friend. Numerous bullets had shattered his car's windscreen. Fortunately, Finley only suffered minor cuts from the broken glass although his friend was wounded in the wrist. All they could tell the local Kaufman County Sheriff was that they'd caught a glimpse of a man with a raised gun, but could not identify him.

Detectives still hunting the killer of Rozanne contacted the Kaufman County authorities to see if there was a link between the two crimes. The local sheriff was convinced that Finley and his friend had stumbled upon a drug deal or some poachers who'd turned their gun on the two men.

So once again the investigation into the murder of Rozanne Gailiunas fizzled out.

Cut to two more years later – in March 1988. Detectives get

a call from a very frightened woman asking for a meeting to discuss the case. She tells police that Richard Finley's former wife, Joy Aylor, planned the Rozanne murder. The tipster – one of Aylor's relatives called Marilyn Andrews – also claimed that Aylor was behind the gun attack on her former husband in 1986. During her interview with detectives, Andrews claims she delivered the money which paid for the Rozanne slaying to a man she now feared was about to kill her because she knew too much.

Andrews explained how she'd taken the money to a designated spot where it had later been picked up. But afterwards she got a call from the man who was supposed to have taken the envelope saying he'd been keeping an eye on her and because she was so pretty he wanted to date her. Within days a romance had developed between Andrews and the hired gun who'd shot and killed Rozanne Gailiunas.

Andrews named the hitman as Robert Cheshire, who'd even bragged to his beautiful young lover about the numerous other people he'd been hired to 'rub out'. Detectives promised Andrews round-the-clock police protection and devised a plan to trap the killer. She would meet him with a concealed microphone to record their entire conversation.

The first encounter in a restaurant was a disaster because background noise drowned out the recorded conversation. Then they agreed to meet in a motel room. Just a few yards away, investigators hid in a van with tape recorders and video cameras running. Soon they'd gathered enough evidence to show that Aylor had taken out contracts on both Rozanne and her own husband Richard Finley. So-called hitman Cheshire was arrested, but insisted he didn't carry out the actual hit and pointed the finger at a number of other middlemen involved in the crime.

Detectives then tape-recorded phone calls between Marilyn Andrews and Aylor. At one stage Andrews says, 'I got one thing that still bothers me.'

'What?'

'Why didn't you get rid of Richard Finley first?'

'I don't know,' Aylor responded. 'Stupid, wasn't it? I thought about that, too. It would have been a lot better.'

In another comment on tape, Aylor told Andrews: 'I paid for it. Really, I have paid for it, not only monetarily but mentally, I've paid for this.'

Joy Aylor was then picked up for questioning by investigators and taken to a local police station. At first the pretty blonde Aylor shrugged off the accusations by claiming Marilyn Andrews was mentally disturbed. Without a full confession from Aylor, the detectives were left with no choice but to release her because she had never actually said on tape that she'd had Rozanne killed.

Months of cat-and-mouse games between detectives and Aylor followed. The murder team tried to confirm the identity of the hitman through a chain of sleazy middlemen, each of whom blamed the next one for the actual hit. But eventually, police established that the last man to receive cash, along with a photo and the address of Rozanne, for the contract hit was an insurance appraiser called Andy Hopper. He had no major criminal record, but was heavily involved in trafficking marijuana. Hopper still retained his full-time job as

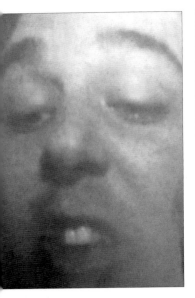

Top left: Neil Markley, 19, took his love affair with middle-aged Julie Cheema to the limits.

Top right: Julie Cheema's marriage was crumbling.

Bottom: The off-licence in Hounslow, Middlesex, where Julie and her husband came to blows.

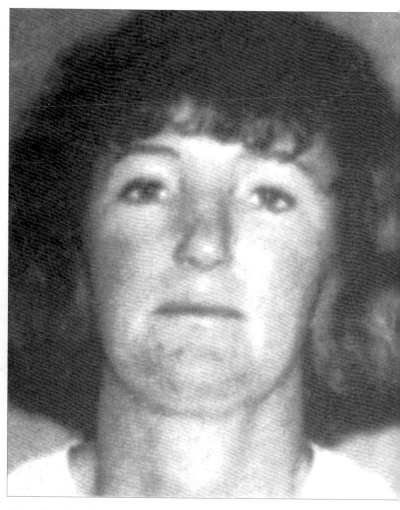

Diana Bogdanoff's addiction to sex proved fatal.

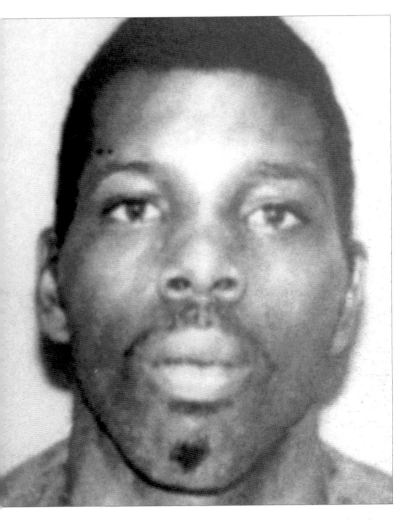

rian Stafford saw himself as a big-time criminal.

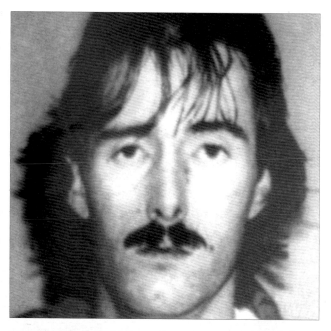

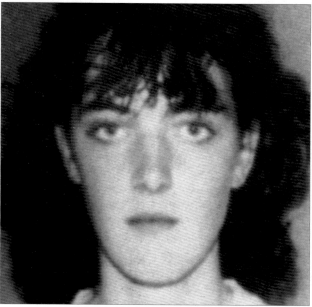

Top: Ricky Rogers was weak and smitten.

Bottom: Stephanie Allen was the daughter from hell.

In 2000, underworld kingpin Kenneth Noye was jailed for the roadrage killing of a motorist on the M25. Months later the chief prosecution witness at that trial was killed by a hitman in a Kent car park.

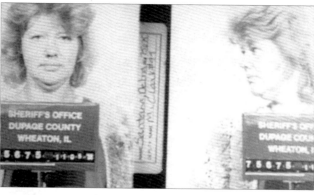

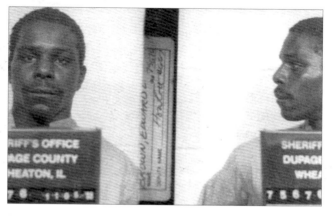

Judy Benkowski (*top*) endured a miserable married life until her friends Debra Santana (*middle*) and Eddie Brown (*bottom*) came to the rescue.

dy Benkowski's marriage to Clarence Jeske was the dream ending to her
ppalling story.

Police Detective Tom Gorniak felt more sympathy for the killers than hitman victim Clarence Benkowski.

an appraiser although police suspected it was nothing more than a 'front job'.

Naturally, Andy Hopper denied all knowledge of the Gailiunas killing when approached at his home. He then excused himself to take a phone call and promptly ran out the back door. Over the following few weeks, detectives tracked Hopper through the Midwest and West of America but he always managed to stay one step ahead of them.

Back in Dallas, detectives believed they still had enough evidence to prosecute Aylor, Marilyn Andrews and four of the alleged middlemen involved in setting up the hit. So on 19 September 1988, all six were indicted to face criminal proceedings. Aylor was charged with capital murder and conspiracy to commit capital murder in the death of Rozanne Gailiunas plus solicitation to commit capital murder on the life of her ex-husband, Richard Finley. The other suspects were indicted on conspiracy charges, two of them – brothers Gary and Buster Matthews – were charged in connection with the 1986 attempted shooting of Finley. Joy Aylor was arrested and taken to Richardson police station but later released on bail having maintained her complete silence.

Meanwhile the hunt for hitman Andy Hopper intensified and, in December 1988, detectives and FBI agents nabbed the alleged triggerman when he returned to the Dallas area to meet a girlfriend. Hopper denied the killing, just like all the other 'go-betweens'. He claimed he'd paid yet another man – a drug dealer from Houston whom he only knew as 'Renfro' – $1,500 to do the job.

Hopper told detectives he'd met Renfro at a drugs and

sex party held at a friend's apartment in Dallas, and later Renfro confirmed to him that the hit on Rozanne had been carried out. Police didn't believe Hopper's story, but the only way they could disprove it was to find Renfro. A woman who was present when Hopper claimed he met Renfro recalled that he'd been busted for drugs in the Highland Park area of Dallas.

Investigators then dug up a mugshot of Renfro Stevenson and showed it to Hopper who immediately cracked and confessed to carrying out the hit himself. In a video-taped statement, Hopper revealed all the details of that night seven years earlier when he'd murdered Rozanne Gailiunas. He even said he'd stolen a .25 automatic from a friend's apartment and then purchased rope, surgical gloves and a potted plant before driving to Rozanne's house.

Hopper then rang the doorbell and gained entry by producing that potted plant and pretending to be a florist. Hopper pulled out the .25 and ordered Rozanne to disrobe and lie face down on the bed, where he tied her up with the rope. When Rozanne began sobbing, Hopper grabbed some tissues from the bedside table and rammed them down her throat. Then he found a belt, placed it around her neck and started strangling her. But Rozanne thrashed around so violently that she managed to free one arm. Hopper shoved a pillow over her head and fired two shots point-blank through the pillow.

Hopper had no idea that Rozanne's four-year-old son was fast asleep in the next room. Hopper also insisted in his statement that he didn't know who ordered the hit. He was jailed without bond on a charge of capital murder.

On 7 May 1990, Joy Aylor failed to turn up at a pre-trial hearing set in order to choose a jury for her coming trial. It then emerged she'd been collecting vast amounts of cash through withdrawals from her bank and selling stocks and other holdings. Investigators also discovered that Aylor and 45-year-old Dallas attorney Ted Bakersfield – arrested on a federal narcotics charge the previous March – had been seen together after they met when she was looking to hire a new attorney to defend her.

Bakersfield recommended that Aylor stick to her original lawyer but the two began a romance. Now associates said they were convinced the couple had fled to Mexico. One friend then admitted dropping off the couple at a car dealership in the nearby town of Cheyenne where Bakersfield splashed out $7,800 on a second-hand jeep, using his real name in the transaction. Authorities began tracking the two fugitives across several western states. In Montana, the pair registered their jeep and picked up local licence plates. It seemed as if they were now heading north for Canada and eventually emerged near Vancouver, British Columbia, where they booked into a remote motel under the name of 'Mr and Mrs John Storms'.

Bakersfield checked out of the motel alone on 11 June and even claimed a partial refund because he'd paid until 14 June. Aylor had already left. The following day a motel clerk contacted local police after seeing an item about the couple on local TV. Later that same day, Bakersfield phoned the motel to see if he'd had any calls. The clerk pretended that an unnamed woman had called for him. Bakersfield presumed Aylor had been in touch. He was so pleased he left the name and phone number of the hotel he'd checked into in rural Osoyoos, British Columbia.

Less than an hour later, eight armed police officers surrounded the premises and burst into Bakersfield's room. He surrendered without a struggle and agreed to return to the United States voluntarily. He was immediately transferred to Spokane, Washington, and then flown to Dallas in the custody of a US marshal.

But there was still no sign of Aylor. Bakersfield claimed she'd walked out on him after an argument. He said he'd even considered suicide before being arrested and blamed all his troubles on his cocaine addiction. He also professed his undying love for Joy Aylor and insisted he was only trying to protect her. FBI agents ran a check of airline flights out of Vacouver Airport and discovered that Aylor had taken a flight to Mexico City on 7 June. Investigators immediately headed south of the border.

In August 1990, Aylor's former husband Richard Finley filed a lawsuit against his missing wife. A newspaper article about the lawsuit was read by a woman who'd just arrived back in Dallas from Mexico. The photo looked just like the woman she'd roomed with who went under a different name. Both had attended a Spanish-language school in Cuernavaca, Mexico. However, when investigators contacted the school they discovered that Aylor hadn't returned for the new term despite registering for it. The Rozanne murder squad from Richardson, Texas, and the FBI then issued an appeal to law enforcement agencies across the world, including Interpol in Europe.

It wasn't until March 1991 that an anonymous tipster told detectives Aylor was using the name Elizabeth Sharp and renting a villa just outside the city of Nice, on the French Riviera. She gave English lessons to local people to earn a living – and she'd acquired for herself an American boyfriend called Albert Neilsen.

Neilsen is suspected of being that tipster because he fled the area minutes before Aylor's arrest on Saturday, 16 March. Aylor insisted her name was Elizabeth Sharp but when authorities made it clear they were fully aware of her past she confessed to her true identity. Aylor was transferred to a local jail where she made a feeble attempt to kill herself by slashing both her wrists, but was immediately rushed to hospital where doctors said her wounds were not deep enough to be life-threatening.

Back in Dallas, investigators began the long and arduous process of extraditing Aylor from France. France's extradition treaty with the US specifically contained a provision protecting capital murder suspects from being extradited because France did not carry out the death penalty. Dallas County prosecutors eventually requested that Aylor be extradited on charges that were not capital cases and assured French authorities she would not be put to death if found guilty. But they still refused to confirm when the extradition would take place which dashed any hopes of trying Aylor before her other co-defendants.

Back in Dallas, jury selection for the trial of so-called triggerman Andy Hopper went ahead. It took six months to seat the panel and another six weeks for the actual trial, making it one of the longest criminal proceedings in Texan history. Hopper effectively convicted himself thanks to his candid, videotaped confession in which he coldly recited all the appalling details of how he murdered Rozanne Gailiunas.

The jury even heard Hopper admit standing over Rozanne's nude and bound body as it lay on the bed and masturbating before strangling her with the belt and then firing two point-blank shots into her head. One of Hopper's jail inmates told the court that he'd confessed to the slaying while they shared a cell. Another friend of the alleged hitman testified that Hopper wrote a letter to him admitting to the murder and showing little remorse for his crimes.

Hopper was found guilty of capital murder, which mandated that he be sentenced to death by lethal injection. The verdict was immediately appealed to the Texas Court of Criminal Appeals.

Meanwhile Joy Aylor remained incarcerated on the French Riviera thanks to highly complex extradition proceedings. It wasn't until November 1993 that the French officially accepted assurance that she would not be put to death if found guilty. US marshals escorted Aylor back to Dallas County to stand trial – 11 years after the original slaying. When she arrived at Dallas-Fort Worth International Airport the once attractive blonde housewife looked drawn and gaunt after so many years on the run.

Jury selection for Aylor's trial finally got under way in May 1994. Assistant District Attorney Kevin Chapman predicted a complex legal battle. 'She started it,' he said. 'She's the one that gave it [the murder] all life. But she's the farthest from the gun.'

Aylor's trial began on 1 August 1994, before Dallas County state district judge Pat McDowell. It was screened live on Court TV. A dishevelled Aylor was shackled at the ankles when she shuffled into the court and immediately entered a 'not guilty' plea. Millions of Americans watched as prosecutors began their case by using two side-by-side projectors – featuring on the left an image of Aylor, the beautiful, blonde and suntanned wife, and on the right screen photos of people and places linked to the case flashed by in sequence. Prosecutor Chapman then outlined the deadly chain of events.

He told the jury that tape recordings of telephone conversations between Aylor and Marilyn Andrews would corroborate the prosecution case. Chapman also told the court that Aylor fled the country because of her fear of being convicted on the murder charge. A stream of witnesses for the prosecution then gave evidence, including officials who arrived at the murder scene, a doctor at the hospital where Rozanne was taken and the medical examiner who performed the autopsy on her body. Then came Albert Neilsen, who'd been living with Aylor in France at the time of her arrest. He'd only been apprehended on a federal fugitive warrant days before the trial began.

Neilsen said that Aylor admitted her role in the slaying. She even told him that she wanted her ex-husband's girlfriend dead so she could reclaim him and the money she believed he'd taken from their joint bank accounts. Aylor also told her lover that she'd had to pay $15,000 blackmail money to Robert Cheshire, who'd originally arranged the hit on Rozanne Gailiunas. Neilsen also admitted taking $200,000 belonging to Joy Aylor from banks in Switzerland and Mexico, which he used to travel the world as a fugitive following Aylor's 1991 arrest. He used most of the cash to buy and later sell a $185,000 sailing boat.

Aylor's defence team branded Neilsen completely unreliable and claimed that his testimony was part of a plea-bargaining deal on federal charges of passport fraud and concealing a fugitive. 'He's a desperate man,' Aylor's attorney told the court. 'I'd expect him to say anything.'

Then came the transcripts of phone conversations between Aylor and Marilyn Andrews in which Aylor said she was stupid not to have her former husband killed as well. Prosecutors also played the tape of a later meeting in a noisy restaurant between Aylor and Andrews. At one stage, Aylor talked about the man she hired for the killing. 'He didn't know who I was at the time,' she said. 'He did not even know who paid to kill her.'

Then one of the middlemen involved in commissioning the hit told the court how he gave triggerman Hopper the money, directions and a photo of the victim. This was followed by testimony from police officers involved in the investigation and subsequent worldwide hunt for Aylor. One veteran Dallas detective described the case as 'Dallas's most complicated murder case'.

The defence team then surprised the court by deciding not to call any witnesses. Closing arguments from attorneys were expected to begin on 15 August, but prosecutors then asked the judge to allow them to reopen testimony in the trial. They wanted Aylor's former lover Ted Bakersfield to take the stand. Three years earlier, he'd pleaded guilty to cocaine charges and been given a 15-year sentence. But he'd been suddenly released in December 1993 after his sentence was reduced to four years, thanks to his co-operation with the Richardson investigators probing Rozanne's murder.

Bakersfield had not been called earlier in case he was needed to rebut any of the defence witnesses but, once it was clear they were not calling anyone, Bakersfield was introduced to the court. He described his love affair with Aylor and how they had several conversations about her involvement in the murder and plans to flee the United States. Bakersfield found it hard to reconcile the woman he'd loved with the cold-hearted killer behind that hit on Rozanne Gailiunas.

But he did recall going to a shooting range where he allowed Aylor to test-fire a new 9mm handgun. She aimed the weapon at a mesquite tree and emptied the clip. Then Aylor handed him back the gun, smiled and said, 'I should've used this on Rozanne.'

Bakersfield also testified that Aylor showed no remorse over the killing she'd commissioned. 'She said if she had to do it all over again, she'd do it differently,' he said. 'She'd do it herself.' He recalled that Aylor once told him that guilt 'was a wasted emotion that could be dealt with under any circumstances and should not be carried around'.

Bakersfield even told the court that Aylor had asked him about finding someone to kill Marilyn Andrews after she tipped off the police. Aylor thought that if Andrews 'was removed' any tape-recorded testimony might not be admissible in court. 'The best defence is a good offence,' Bakersfield quoted his former lover as saying.

Summing up, prosecutors stressed Aylor's behaviour as she fled police and pointed out the damaging content of various tape-recorded conversations. Defence attorneys claimed that Aylor didn't hire anyone to carry out the hit but did employ Robert Cheshire to rough up her ex-husband. They insisted the death of Rozanne Gailiunas was the result of an overzealous hitman.

Prosecutors dismissed the claims by recalling the tape-recorded comment Aylor made to Marilyn Andrews that, 'He [Robert Cheshire] did not know who paid to kill her.' Assistant District Attorney Chapman pointed out to the jury: 'Does that sound like a woman who ordered eggs and bacon?'

On 18 August 1994, the jury deliberated for just two-and-a-half hours before finding Joy Aylor guilty of capital murder. She was given life imprisonment because the French authorities had only extradited her on condition the death penalty was not instated. Aylor showed no emotion as she was led away to a Texas Department of Corrections jail.

Her last lover, Albert Neilsen, later pleaded guilty to nine charges, including helping hide Aylor while she was on the run and passport fraud. The judge announced an adjournment on sentencing. Middlemen Buster Matthews and Gary Matthews were given life sentences for their attempted shooting of Richard Finley.

Chapter Eleven:

STAND BY YOUR MAN

Twelve-year-old Michelle Samarasinha kissed her mother goodbye at the breakfast table and headed out into the bitterly cold January morning. She was to meet her father at the garage behind their home, where he was warming up the car to take her to school. All along Demesne Road, in the Surrey commuter belt town of Wallington, just south of London, businessmen and women were coming out of their neat, suburban houses and heading briskly towards the nearby railway station.

As the schoolgirl walked around the side of the row of houses to meet her father, she wondered why his car wasn't out of the garage yet. Michelle headed towards the alleyway which provided a speedy cut-through to the lock-up garage. Then she spotted a group of people gathered around something on the pavement. One woman with a dog on the end of a lead was speaking to the others. She was saying, 'I thought he was drunk or something, and then he collapsed.'

Just then little Michelle peered through a gap in the crowd and noticed a man's shiny shoes and grey trouser legs. The pair of Aviator sunglasses, with one lens broken, lying on the pavement sent a shiver down the spine of Michelle. She started shaking. In the distance, the loud wail of police sirens got closer and closer.

Michelle finally plucked up the courage to look down at the figure on the pavement properly. A woman was crouching over her beloved father, giving him mouth-to-mouth resuscitation. She only pulled back as two paramedics forced a pathway through the crowd. Then Michelle noticed her father's pullover was soaked in blood.

Nimal Samarasinha – known as Sam to everyone – died before the ambulance could even get him to hospital. He'd bled to death from a single knife wound to the heart. It later transpired he'd been stabbed as he went to open the door of his garage. Then he'd managed to stagger a few yards before crashing on to the pavement.

Police immediately sealed off the area and began interviewing witnesses and residents. One man claimed he saw two or three men in a white Ford Escort, who'd driven off so fast that the witness had presumed they were late for work. He couldn't even provide a description of their clothes, but he did recall that they all looked 'Indian or something'. He hadn't even managed to get a note of any part of the car number plate. Detectives were baffled by the cold-blooded nature of the attack in a quiet suburban street. Was it a botched robbery? But it was so unusual to die from one single thrust of a knife and, in any case, few muggers ever resorted to murder.

Detective Inspector Tony Kirby then went to call on the grieving widow and child of the deceased. He was expecting a lot of tears, especially because of the violent, sudden nature of Samarasinha's death. Victim's wife Florence Samarasinha answered the front door wearing dark glasses, elegant clothes and fashionable slingbacks, and dabbing her eyes with a handkerchief.

It was that style which had so impressed Sri Lankan-born Sam when the couple first met in Africa in 1978. He was 22 and had just been posted to Nigeria with Bristow Helicopters. Sam took great pleasure in bringing Florence back with him to London at the end of his Nigerian contract. However, Sam's extremely conservative family were horrified when he announced he was marrying an African woman rather than someone from his own cultural background.

Sam's parents even made some discreet enquiries about Florence's background. But communications between Nigeria and the UK were not good and they found precious little information about her family or circumstances. They just hoped and prayed that the romance would fizzle out before the couple could take their marriage vows. But Sam remained besotted with Florence and the wedding quickly went ahead.

Florence knew her husband's family didn't approve of her. But she ignored it all. Her first job in London was as an administrator for Brent Council. Then in 1985 she beat dozens of rival applicants to an important administration job at Croydon Council, in south London. Soon she was head of the housing benefits department, with a staff of 80, earning £30,000 a year. She was the first black woman to become a senior official at Croydon Council.

All this apparent success left Detective Inspector Kirby wondering why the family hadn't moved to a more expensive house. This one was extremely modestly furnished. Kirby noted daughter Michelle's private school uniform and Florence's immaculate Mercedes in front of the house. But apart from those two extravagances, the family weren't exactly big spenders.

However, Kirby was already aware there had been some serious domestic problems between Sam and Florence in recent months. Police had been called to the house four times by Florence, including one incident which resulted in Sam getting a nasty cut on his head. On another occasion, officers arrived to find the couple arguing in the street. Another time Florence claimed her husband had attacked her with a knife. Officers even told Sam – who always denied his wife's claims – to go and sleep at another address until things cooled down. But when police urged Florence to get a legal injunction out against her husband, she refused.

Back in their Wallington home, DI Kirby listened intently as Florence suddenly made a revealing comment: 'I don't know if I should be telling you this, but my husband was involved in the drugs business,' she sniffed. 'I never knew what was going on, but I know there had been some threats against him. He used to get these strange phone calls at night.'

Moments later, Florence burst into tears as if she was trying to emphasise the point. DI Kirby sensed she was acting. But it wasn't that surprising if she'd been subjected to the alleged spousal abuse, which had prompted all those earlier calls to the house. Maybe she was just pleased that he couldn't bully her any more?

But when investigators began checking on murder victim Sam's background, a completely different picture emerged. No one had a bad word to say about him. Friends and associates described him as a kind, thoughtful man who doted on only-child Michelle. She believed her father to be one of the most gentle people in the world. Sam didn't even like watching police shows on TV because he found them too violent. He adored sport but thought football was turning increasingly rough and so preferred cricket.

Most mornings, Sam would drop his daughter at school and then make the 45-minute drive to Bristow Helicopters in Redhill, Surrey, where he was an aviation engineer. During the school run, father and child always had the most enjoyable conversations – something that Michelle later said she would never forget.

However, on the day before he was killed, Sam had revealed to little Michelle that he and her mother were about to split up. He told his daughter: 'You're going to have to make a very difficult choice. You have to decide which of us you're going to live with.'

'With you, Daddy. I want to live with you.'

Little did either of them realise that would never happen.

Head of the murder investigation, Detective Superintendent Brian Younger and the rest of his colleagues soon concluded that Sam was the type of man who really did not deserve to die. And every one of his friends said there was no way he'd ever been involved in the shady world of drug dealing. In that case why was Florence trying to suggest it?

Back at the family's Wallington home, DI Kirby went back to Florence to gently confront her about those earlier drugs claims. She immediately responded by insisting her late husband must have been dealing in 'something bad – pornography or smuggling'. Over the following few days, Florence poured out theory after theory as to why her husband was killed. But none of it added up.

Florence also boasted to DI Kirby about her powerful job at Croydon Council and how she had an honours degree from Cambridge. Later that day, Kirby got his office to check out her qualifications and they turned out to be bogus. Even Florence's seven GCSE 'O' levels and five 'A' levels in her application for the Croydon job were non-existent – as were a bunch of glowing references from her previous job at Brent Council.

When Kirby went back and confronted Florence, she dismissed all her lies as irrelevant, saying her employers in Croydon said she was doing a splendid job. But her colleagues reported that Florence rarely completed more than half a day of work at a time and often only made a brief appearance in the morning before putting on her coat and leaving. She told staff she was out investigating bogus claims for housing benefits. Florence insisted she often ended up working in the evenings to catch these money-grabbing cheats.

Then investigators discovered that, despite her high salary, Florence was constantly in debt. She'd even borrowed money from junior colleagues and recently added £5,000 to the mortgage on the family home. She also had a £5,000 claim against an insurance company rejected because it was bogus. And she was currently more than £34,000 in debt.

DS Brian Younger attended the funeral service for Sam at Croydon Crematorium a few days later and got the distinct impression that the murdered man was trying to tell him something. Sam had been so wary of an early, unexpected death he'd carefully written out the directions for his funeral, right down to the music, which turned out to be Tammy Wynette's 'Stand By Your Man'. Younger later recalled, 'Standing there listening to it. I could only think it was a bit ironic.'

So it was no surprise that the first real break in the case came from the victim himself. It emerged that Sam – a meticulous character – had made an appointment for himself and Florence to see a local social services official to decide who should get custody of Michelle in the event of their legal separation. Sam had made precise notes in preparation for the meeting. He'd even written that Florence's career at Croydon Council was a complete sham. He also branded her an unfit mother for their child.

And when Sam had uncovered that Florence was heavily in debt he'd presumed she was having an affair, so he'd even hired a private detective called Yousef Ghida to shadow her every movement. Ghida soon reported back that she was spending all her money on gambling. She adored amusement arcades and would spend hours each day on the fruit machines.

Rudy Drummond, manager of the MDJ amusement arcade on Church Street, Croydon, near Wallington, later told police: 'She was in here four days a week. At first it would only be for an hour or two. Then it was three, four, five hours. Sometimes all day. Now and then she'd be up to about £30 or so. But I'd say she was losing an average of 50 quid a day. Several hundred pounds a week, anyway.' Florence was losing something in the region of £1,000 a week at various arcades across south London.

But then private eye Ghida came up with some even more dramatic news: Florence was working for the Effleurage Escort Agency as a hooker to try and pay off her debts. It then dawned on Sam that his wife was capable of *anything*. He hoped all these revelations would help him win custody of Michelle, so he instructed private eye Ghida to get some solid evidence which could be used in a court of law if necessary.

A few weeks later Ghida returned with secretly filmed videotape of him going to an appointment with Florence as a prospective client. On the film, Florence – wearing just a pair of skimpy white panties – tells Ghida she's 'new in this business' and is working to pay off some debts. 'If there is anything you want me to do, just say so.' Moments later Ghida pretends he can't perform and apologises, saying, 'I've lost my bottle.' Then Florence asks him, 'Would you like a massage?' He politely declines, puts on his clothes and takes back part of the £100 he's paid her.

Sam felt humiliated and appalled as he watched the video, but realised it was crucial evidence, along with her gambling, to put before a judge to convince him that Florence was an unfit mother. Later that same day, Sam confronted his wife about her secret life as a vice girl. Florence accused her husband of lying and told him there was no way she would leave the house and abandon her child. She knew then she would have to do something very drastic.

During that summer of 1991, Florence met a cleaning contractor called Simon Wash at a neighbour's drinks party. He clearly found her attractive and was extremely sympathetic when she told him that her husband regularly beat her up. But Wash's ears pricked up even more when Florence mentioned that she handed out cleaning contracts at Croydon Council.

'Come to my office and we can talk about some contracts due for renewal,' she told Wash. He wanted to impress Florence enough to ensure she gave him the business, so he decided to take an associate called Gerry Smithers, a nightclub bouncer and weightlifter, with him to the meeting. Florence gave the muscle merchant a friendly 'Hmmmmm!' as Smithers walked in. 'You're a big boy. You might be able to help me.' Smithers offered to provide Florence protection from her brutal, violent husband. He even said he might 'have a word with him' if necessary.

While Simon Wash's main priority was discussing cleaning contracts, Florence had other ideas on her mind. 'My husband's been beating me up all the time and he stole £350,000 from the textile firm we own,' she told the two men within minutes of their arrival. The 'textile firm' was a figment of Florence's colourful imagination. She continued, 'He's even tried to kill me, can you imagine? Someone fired a gun at me not far from home. I know he hired somebody to do it.' Then she paused for a moment before ever-so-casually asking, 'Would you kill my husband for me?'

Wash and Smithers coughed and spluttered and a long silence filled the room. Then Wash chipped in, 'Wouldn't it be a better idea if you moved into a hotel for a while? Let things cool down a bit?'

But all that did was send Florence into floods of tears. 'You don't understand. He's molested our daughter. You wouldn't believe it. He had one of his uncles rape me once, and,' she sobbed,' he stood there and watched.'

Smithers handed Florence a huge, manly handkerchief and assured her, 'Don't cry, love. We'll sort it all out for you.' As they left the building both men shrugged their shoulders with bewilderment at what they'd just heard. It seemed a bit of a steep price to pay for a cleaning contract.

But Florence was determined to get what she wanted. Next day she phoned hardman Gerry Smithers and told him that her husband was in the aviation business and could get hold of a private plane and fly him and their daughter out of the country at a moment's notice. 'Oh, Gerry, you've got to do something for me. Even if you can't do it, you must know someone who could help.'

So when Gerry Smithers read that Florence's husband had been stabbed dead in an alley behind their house that icy January morning, he felt compelled to visit his local police station. Detective Superintendent Younger later explained: 'He was prepared to put pen to paper.' It was the turning point in the case. Smithers' statement was enough for detectives to get a warrant for the arrest of Florence, who was then charged with soliciting murder.

Then arcade owner Rudy Drummond came forward and told officers he'd slung Florence out of his premises after she kept talking about her husband's cruelty and how she'd one day kill her husband. Drummond never forgot the phrase she used: 'I'd take a knife and push it in.'

Detectives then located more than 20 men who'd paid for sex with Florence. This wasn't a crime in itself, but investigators wanted to know if she'd ever asked any of these men to arrange a hit on her husband.

Police then interviewed a man called John Cheetham, who was chairman of the the Citizens' Police Consultative Committee and knew Florence through her work for Croydon Council. Flamboyant Cheetham – who favoured bow-ties and rimless specs, and had vast protruding Bugs Bunny teeth – saw himself as a prominent do-gooder in the community. He was a paid official of Church Action with the Unemployed and chairman of a Croydon voluntary group. He described Florence as a charming, bright woman who was very good at her work – which seemed to contradict everything else the police had heard.

So for the moment, detectives had failed to find out who Florence had paid to kill her husband.

Then four months later – just before Florence's committal hearing – Cheetham contacted detectives and said he'd been 'less than frank' about his connection to Florence. Cheetham, 47 and single, admitted using hookers from time to time and even boasting to them about his police connections as well as knowing SAS people trained to kill. So one prostitute friend of his, called Jacky Bartlett, took it upon herself to take Florence with her when she went to Cheetham's home in December 1991.

Within minutes Florence poured out all her most outrageous lies about 'abusive' husband Sam and his plans to steal their daughter. Florence ended the conversation by saying to Cheetham, 'I'd be willing to pay £500 to have somebody do away with him.'

Cheetham was rather taken aback and pointed out, 'It's not as easy as that. Why don't you think of some other option like divorce?'

'Are you kidding?' responded Florence. 'He's so clever, he's bound to find some way to get custody of our daughter.'

'If I can think of someone I'll let you know,' said Cheetham, who later told police that the two met again a few weeks afterwards, but he still wasn't able to find her a hitman.

So by the time Florence Samarasinha appeared in the dock of the Old Bailey in December 1993, police still had no idea who'd killed her husband for her. For important legal reasons Florence was charged with murder as well as soliciting murder. For without a murder charge, information about the actual murder would have been kept out of the trial so it didn't prejudice any future trial. That might have helped Florence escape justice. Now with the murder charge the jury could hear the full sordid details behind Florence's many attempts to recruit a hitman.

Florence, now 41, looked distraught and stressed as witness after witness took the Old Bailey stand and revealed their role in the case. The court was even shown the videotape of private eye Yousef Ghida hiring Florence as a hooker. Client John Cheetham was given a rough ride by the prosecution after admitting he'd been 'economical with the truth' during his first interview with the police. He explained to the court, 'My concern was that my involvement with prostitutes for paid sex would become public.'

Outspoken defence counsel Michael Mansfield then emphasised to the court Cheetham's sexual peccadilloes. Cheetham eventually lost his cool and snapped back, 'Your questioning this afternoon seems to have focused more on my involvement with prostitutes than the murder of Mr Samarasinha.'

Club bouncer Gerry Smithers flew back from his new home in Texas to testify at the Old Bailey. He admitted making 'a few suggestions' to Florence. These included faking her husband's death as a suicide or leaving drugs beside his body to suggest an underworld killing. Smithers even alleged to the court that one supposed hitman had been paid to kill Sam and then disappeared without carrying out the job. The police were never able to find out any further evidence of this.

Naturally when Florence took the stand, she insisted that every witness had lied. Then she was asked why Smithers went to the police about her.

'I don't know why he did it,' she responded. 'But he's lying. It's not me who's lying.'

Florence also branded arcade owner Rudy Drummond a liar. 'I never said that the best thing I could do was to stick a knife in him. That's a lie.'

She even denied working as a prostitute, insisting she was

doing undercover work to expose housing fraud as part of her job with Croydon Council. But surely she'd tell her colleagues about such a sensitive aspect of her work? 'I did not tell anyone I was behaving as a masseuse or taking my clothes off,' she replied. 'But I told them I was handling an investigation and it was very dangerous.'

Florence also claimed that she'd put down all those false qualifications on her application form for the Croydon job 'because I didn't really want the job'. She insisted she'd made sure she was the last person interviewed so she wouldn't get the job.

But despite all the counterclaims and lies there was precious little substantial evidence linking Florence to the actual hit on her husband. Even the couple's bank records showed no evidence of a large withdrawal of cash. Detective Younger told the court: 'We were looking for a large sum of money being paid out. But no matter how much we trawled we didn't find it. We can only figure she had a large amount of cash.'

So the police were extremely relieved when the Old Bailey jury found Florence guilty of soliciting her husband's murder by a majority 10–2 verdict. Then followed an 11–1 majority on the murder charge which was even more unexpected. Florence let out an emphatic 'No' from the dock after the verdicts were announced. Mr Justice Phillips sentenced Florence to life imprisonment after telling the court the killing was 'not committed in the heat of the moment, but was deliberately planned and carried out in cold blood.' Florence insisted she would mount an appeal against the jury's verdict. She had the incentive of a

£190,000 life insurance payout if she could overturn the Old Bailey decision.

But ultimately, more than anything else, Florence Samarasinha's unsubtle efforts to get her husband killed helped to convict her. As DS Younger pointed out after the case, 'She might as well have gone around with a loud hailer asking if anyone was willing to murder her husband.'

Florence went off to prison still insisting she was an innocent victim. And her daughter Michelle also believes it to this day. As DS Younger explained: 'She lost one parent; she didn't want to lose two.' Michelle was placed with some of Florence's friends following her mother's arrest and refused to accept that one parent had murdered the other. Michelle even believed the police were the real villains. 'Some day I hope she discovers the truth,' Younger later explained.

Now with her mother incarcerated, Michelle is left with little else but the memories of when they were together as a family. She'd certainly never forget her father's last day on this planet. How he'd reminded her not to forget her homework. How the front door slammed behind him as he went out to get the car to take her to school. How her mother sat in the kitchen with a distant, glazed expression on her face drinking a cup of coffee and trying to read the newspaper. Michelle knew their marriage had been falling apart but why did he have to die?

Chapter Twelve:

SEX IN THE SUBURBS

Noeleen Hendley's affair with the handsome father of her daughter-in-law inevitably ended up involving a number of useful accomplices. Eventually, she even told her own 22-year-old daughter Michelle who, rather conveniently, happened to be moving down to London to live. That gave Noeleen the perfect excuse for even more clandestine meetings with her skilful widowed lover. 'Just off to London to stay with Michelle for the weekend,' she told husband Tony in the second week of September 1991. 'You don't mind do you, love? Bit of shopping and a good natter. Just the two of us.'

Terry nodded his head and waved goodbye to his loving wife on the doorstep of their modest home on the outskirts of Derby as Noeleen took off in a taxi for the station. Noeleen didn't bother catching a train because lover Terry McIntosh was waiting in the station car park with his camper van.

Within an hour they were heading into the Welsh mountains and a picturesque bed and breakfast break where the couple signed themselves in, naturally, as Mr and Mrs McIntosh. That afternoon they walked hand in hand through the hills, stopped by the side of fresh water streams and even made passionate love under an oak tree. Noeleen and Terry never wanted their love for each other to end. But was it possible to be together forever?

'There is a way we could make it permanent,' said Terry, as the couple sat at the edge of a noisy stream.

'Don't be daft. There's no future in this,' Noeleen snapped back.

'But if Tony wasn't around…'

'What do you mean? Not around? He's here.'

'What if something were to happen to him?'

'What are you on about?'

'You know. Something…'

'Do you mean if he was struck by lightning or something?' She paused. 'That's not going to happen, Terry.'

'But I know a bloke who…'

Noeleen stopped dead in her tracks as they sat by the side of the stream and looked right into Terry's eyes.

'What bloke?'

'A bloke who'd do anything for the right amount of cash.'

'You're serious, aren't you?' she asked intently.

Terry nodded.

'How much cash?' she asked, carefully.

Tony was surprised Noeleen hadn't laughed in his face.

'Couple of grand, I suppose.'

Just then a broad smile came to Noeleen's face. 'Come off

it, Terry,' she grabbed his hand like a lovesick teenager. 'Come on, race you back to the van.'

But Noeleen had a feeling that Terry was deadly serious and she wanted time to think over his proposition. Over the following few days, she kept waking up in the middle of the night thinking about what life might be like without Tony. Having Terry making warm, passionate love to her seemed so much better a proposition than her current, dull life in the suburbs. Maybe Terry's 'idea' wasn't so crazy after all.

Not long afterwards, Noeleen and Terry met up for yet another secret rendezvous near both their homes in Derby and it quickly became obvious Terry had also been giving the matter a lot of thought.

Terry even named the man 'who'd do it for the cash': Paul Buxton. 'I've known him since we were nippers,' said Terry. 'He owes me five hundred quid does Paul. We'd have to pay him another thousand quid up front. But it's not that much, is it?'

Less than an hour later, Noeleen found herself withdrawing two lots of £250 from two of her building society accounts. What the bloody hell am I doing, she asked herself. But all she could think about was Terry and making passionate love to him for ever and ever.

By the time she handed over the cash to her secret lover, she was shaking like a leaf. However, she did inform him it was all in a plastic bag 'so there'll be no fingerprints'. She can't have been that scared.

Noeleen and Terry then had sex at Terry's place. Noeleen

felt more sexually excited than ever before, knowing that soon he'd have her all to himself.

A few minutes later, Terry got up from the bed to wash himself and he called out to Noeleen: 'I've been thinking about when's the best time to do it.'

Noeleen was admiring herself in the mirror. I haven't got a bad figure for a 46-year-old mum of three, she thought to herself. 'What d'you mean, love?' she asked.

Terry was drying himself with a towel as he walked back into the bedroom. 'You see, I got this plan, like. You know the UCI cinema, don't you?'

'Yeah. Course I do.'

'Well, when you come out of there you have to walk over a piece of waste ground to get back to your place, right?'

Noeleen nodded slowly, not quite sure where all this was leading.

'Well, that's when my man pounces. Bang. Bang. Think about it for a minute, love. This is important.'

Noeleen didn't really want to consider the cold, hard reality of the situation but she eventually agreed. 'Right, I see what you mean.'

Terry continued. 'If you can let me know when you and Tony are going to the pictures, say next Saturday, I can have Paul waiting there. You just give him your bag and jewellery, like it's a robbery. Then he just bashes Tony over the head. It's all over in a flash.'

Noeleen flashed a picture of the attack up in her mind. It was scary, but it forced her to think about a few important issues. 'But how will he know it's us?' she asked.

'Good point. I hadn't thought of that.'

'I know, I'll wear my white trousers and top. I'll be all in white. Then he can't get it wrong. We'll talk about all this later,' added Noeleen, as she looked at the time and realised she needed to get home to make husband Tony his tea.

The following day, Paul Buxton was handed £1,000 in cash as he sat in Terry's red Ford Fiesta in the car park of the Three Horseshoes pub in Morley, near Derby. Buxton stuffed it in his pocket nervously. He'd never done anything like this before in his life and was so worried he'd recruited another mate to help prevent anything going wrong.

A few minutes later, Buxton told his friend: 'I'll sub you £450 now with more to come when the job's completed.' His friend was more than happy with his share.

But the next day when Buxton went to pick up his so-called accomplice, the man lost his nerve. 'Are you fuckin' crazy? Kill some bloke for a few hundred quid. No fuckin' way.'

'But what about the money I gave you?' pleaded Buxton.

'Hard fuckin' luck, mate. You owed me it anyway.'

Later that night, Noeleen and her husband Tony walked out of the cinema and across the wasteland in complete safety. Plan number one had gone completely out of the window.

The next murderous scheme involved Terry taking his old mate Tony out for a drink at the Leather and Lace pub. First he'd drive him into the nearby Cock Pitt island car park. While he was out getting a parking ticket from the machine, Terry's mate Paul Buxton would appear out of nowhere and bash Tony over the head. Terry would then intervene and Buxton would run over Terry's legs while making his escape –

just to convince the cops he was not involved. But that plan bit the dust when kind-hearted Buxton announced he couldn't run over his good friend.

'You're my mate. I can't do it.'

'Get outta here!'

Plan two had been aborted before take-off.

So it was back to plan A – the cinema heist – with one big difference. This time, Terry was to be his friend Paul Buxton's accomplice.

On Saturday, 18 October 1991, Terry parked up his Fiesta at the Garden City pub. Then he and Buxton walked half a mile to the UCI cinema and waited nervously for the crowds to come out. 'Here they come,' said Terry, pulling down a green balaclava helmet that, by pure chance, had been knitted for him by Noeleen, who was now walking arm-in-arm with the man she wanted dead.

But unfortunately the couple were walking in the opposite direction to the plan. The two would-be killers did a quick shuffle and headed off to intersect them. Paul Buxton gripped hard on the piece of armoured cable hidden beneath his coat.

'Good girl,' muttered Terry under his breath as Noeleen followed her earlier instructions and dropped Tony's arm so as to make the attack on him easier to carry out. Just as Paul Buxton stepped forward out of the darkness another man appeared nearby. The murderous moment had once again passed. Yet another mission was aborted.

Naturally, more plans were then discussed including running Tony over in the car park of the Moon pub in nearby

Spondon. But that was abandoned because the lighting was too bright and they might have been spotted by other customers. The next proposal was for Paul Buxton to let himself into the Hendley house one evening while Noeleen was accompanied by Tony to her slimming club. Buxton would then fuse the lights. On arriving home, Noeleen would tell Tony there was a torch under the sink and as he bent down Buxton would use an iron bar to hit over the head in the darkness.

But on 23 October – the night before it was supposed to happen – the phone rang and Tony answered it.

'It's for you, love,' he said, handing the receiver to Noeleen. 'It's someone from the slimming club.'

But in fact it was Paul Buxton.

'It's all off,' he told Noeleen.

'Thanks for letting me know, love,' she said, all cheery and bright as her husband listened nearby. 'See you soon.'

Noeleen was incensed and Terry was so angry with Buxton for backing out that he made Buxton meet Noeleen and him at her home once Tony and her daughter had gone to work. It was the first and only time Buxton actually met Noeleen face to face. 'I want him gone, now,' she hissed at her lover Terry, who said they should give the would-be hitman one final chance.

So yet another plan was set for the following Friday – 25 October. This time Noeleen would let Buxton in through the patio doors while Tony was away attending a colleague's retirement party. Once again, Buxton would tamper with the fuses and then wait with an iron bar for Tony to return. But then Tony went and caught the flu and never left the house for the rest of that week. This was getting beyond a joke.

But determined Noeleen decided the plan should still go ahead. When the lights went out she would send Tony down from his sickbed to repair the fuse and Paul Buxton would be waiting for him. But just as Buxton was about to slip through the open patio doors at about 10pm, the family cat jumped onto his shoulders, scaring the wits out of him so badly that he ran off in a fright.

The plan to kill Tony Hendley had long since turned into a farce. So-called hardman Paul Buxton was such a drip he was scared of cats. Yet despite the warning signs, this murderous trio agreed on one last attempt to kill Tony Hendley and, amazingly, it would come within a whisker of working.

On Friday, 1 November, Noeleen and her accomplices carried out an elaborate plan. It all started that afternoon when Terry drove Noeleen and Tony over to see a house in nearby Oakwood that her son Shane and Terry's daughter Kay were planning to buy together. It seemed perfectly natural that the three parents would go together. Tony even considered Terry to be more his friend than Noeleen's. After all, Terry had helped him lay paving stones in their garden as well as put up a pagoda. Tony felt sorry for Terry since he hadn't got a wife to go home to.

So while the unsuspecting Tony took a look at the back garden of the house being viewed with Shane and Kay, Terry whispered into Noeleen's ear: 'It's on for tonight. Definite.'

Noeleen rolled her eyes as if to say she'd heard it all many times before. But Terry was deadly serious.

Less than an hour later, Terry dropped Tony and Noeleen off at their home in Coniston Crescent and headed in his car for Loscoe where he gave Paul Buxton a stern lecture.

By the time Terry got home early that evening, his daughter Kay pointed out he'd missed his tea and was running late for a meeting he and Shane had arranged with Tony at the Rocket pub.

'Never mind, love. We'll pick up some fish 'n' chips on the way,' replied Terry, who definitely had a lot on his mind.

A few minutes later he bought some food from a local chippie then announced to Shane he'd forgotten to put vinegar on his chips. Instead of returning to the shop, he conveniently popped into Tony and Noeleen's for some vinegar.

Inside the house, Terry told Noeleen: 'It's on. Paul will phone you when he's on his way. Will you be alright?'

Noeleen nodded. 'Course I will. Here, you'd better take a tray to eat those fish and chips or you'll get grease all down the front of you.'

A few minutes later, Shane went into the Rocket pub to get his dad and then dropped the two men off at their favourite watering hole, the Moon. Tony noticed that Terry kept filling his glass up with drink but he put it down to his friend's generosity at the time.

Back at Coniston Crescent, Noeleen had settled in for the evening in her silk pyjamas with a cardigan around her shoulders. Then daughter Dawn came down dressed up for an evening out.

'I'll be home about three or four, Mum, all right?'

'You got a key?'

'Right here.'

'Bye love, have a good time.'

As the door closed behind Dawn, Noeleen checked her handbag to make sure the money was safe. She'd already counted it at least five times: £1,465. This time, she'd got Tony to take it out of the building society after telling him she wanted to buy some British Telecom shares. If things went according to plan there would be another £3,000 for Paul Buxton after Terry sold his house and moved in with Noeleen. Or maybe they'd buy themselves a brand new house well away from Derby. It all sounded so exciting that it helped Noeleen forget about the chilling reality of what was about to occur.

At 10:20pm she nearly jumped out of her skin when the phone rang. 'I'm on my way,' Paul Buxton told her. She parted the curtains slightly as the pre-arranged signal that the coast was clear.

A few minutes later, after putting on her dressing gown, she spotted Buxton walking up the path and hurried to the back to unlock the patio door for him. He looked pale and nervous. Earlier that day, Buxton had even approached a friend and asked him: 'How would you like to waste a bloke in Derby? There's a thousand quid in it for you.' The friend had turned him down flat.

'You going to be alright?' Noeleen asked him.

'Course I am. Where's the ... you-know-what?'

'Here it is.'

Noeleen handed him a rolling pin from the top of the fridge.

'What's up with this fuckin' light,' he said, flicking the switch on and off in the hall.

'I took the bulb out, remember?'

'Oh yeah, sorry.'

'You can see by the light in the bathroom. Come up.'

Noeleen led Buxton to a small sewing room at the front of the house. 'He won't see you here as he comes up the stairs. Just don't make any noise.'

By the time Shane arrived at the Moon at 11:10pm to pick up the two men, Terry was extremely tipsy. Kay and Shane glanced at each other in amusement as their dads laughed and joked in the back of the car on the way home that night.

'You all right?' Terry asked Tony as they stopped to let Tony out at his front gate.

'Abso-fuckin-lootly,' slurred Tony. 'Right as rain..'

Upstairs in the sewing room Paul Buxton, wearing a black balaclava helmet, armed with that rolling pin in his gloved hand, watched Tony stumbling up the garden path. From the car, Terry, Shane and Kay watched as he just managed to close the wrought-iron gate behind him. A few more steps and he was through the side door, which was always left unlocked for him on such occasions.

Noeleen ignored her husband when he mumbled something about making her a cup of tea and stayed wrapped in a duvet on the living room sofa. She heard Tony curse the hall light for not working. Then he began climbing the stairs with great uncertainty. Noeleen crept out into the hall. This time it really was going to happen. They'd be shot of the old bugger for good. The man she'd never really loved, the man who didn't mean anything to her. The man who was rarely capable of making love to her.

Upstairs, Tony stumbled into the toilet. Noeleen looked upwards just as she heard the first blow connect with a sharp crack. Tony cried out. She felt a surge of joy and relief. The blows that followed were softer and more muffled, as if someone was hitting a cushion. Then followed a handful of grunts and cries which seemed to go on forever. That was followed by total silence. A deathly lull.

Noeleen took a deep breath and then spotted the outline of someone creeping quietly down the stairs. She gasped with relief when she realised it was Paul Buxton.

'Is he…?'

'Yes. But it's all gone a bit wrong,' Buxton panted, his eyes wide and bulbous. 'It's a right bloody mess up there. He wouldn't go down easy.' Buxton paused for a moment. 'Have you got it?'

'Here you are,' responded Noeleen, as she took the money from the pocket of her dressing gown and handed it to him.

Just then what felt like a fist smashed into her face and lights flashed in front of her eyes. Her nose immediately throbbed with pain.

'Why d'you do that? You hurt me,' she cried.

'Listen, you say the burglar hit you as he was escaping. Makes it more convincing,' said Buxton. Noeleen had completely forgotten that part of the plan. 'Now, I'd better go back upstairs and make sure the job is done.'

Noeleen heard him open the door to the toilet again and then, to her surprise, there was more thumping. Eventually, Buxton came back downstairs again.

'I never saw a man take such a hiding,' he said in the hallway, looking badly shaken. 'It's all over now. Remember, don't even bring my name into it or you'll be sorry.'

Noeleen, dabbing the blood from her nose, watched as he slipped out through the open patio doors. She knew that now it was her turn to put on a word-perfect performance. She sat herself on the bottom stair, went forward on her knees, then began crawling up the steps, one by one. She expected to see Tony lying there on the landing. Nothing. So, in the faint green glow from the bathroom light, she forced herself to look towards the bedroom.

Then she nearly died of fright. Her husband was standing there, looking straight at her. All she could see was a mass of blood where his face should have been.

'Tony?'

He said nothing. He took a step towards her and put out his hand. He was going to touch her shoulder.

'Oh God!'

She let out a scream, turned and scuttled back down the stairs. It was too late now. She couldn't do anything about it. If she tried to finish him off then the police would know what had happened. And if Paul Buxton couldn't kill him, why on earth would she be able to?

Noeleen had no choice but to follow through with the plan because if he didn't die, her only chance was if the police believed her story that a burglar had slipped into the house without her knowledge. She looked down at the blood staining her pyjama bottoms, ran her fingers through her hair, then pulled open the front door.

'Help me! Please help me!'

It was all a far cry from the day Noeleen and Tony Hendley settled into comfortable middle age in a nice little semi-detached house at 8, Coniston Crescent, in Derby. Back in those days, Tony had just left the army and got himself a good job as Catering Manager for Lubrizol Laboratories so that Noeleen hadn't even had to work. Trouble was that Noeleen wasn't the type to sit around doing nothing. She certainly didn't like to feel too settled.

So she joined the local slimming club at The Guildhall in Derby. And she watched with delight as all her hard effort in the gym and in her diet paid off handsomely. She bought smarter clothes, she tinted her hair an eye-catching blonde. But what people noticed most of all was the change in her personality. Now Noeleen had the confidence to flirt and she was constantly the centre of attention.

Soon she was managing three slimming clubs, all connected to the *Slimming Magazine* organisation and even took members off to conventions as far afield as London and Birmingham. Back at home, the marriage of her son Shane to Kay McIntosh in July 1991 provided wedding photos in which Noeleen outshone the bride. Husband Tony with his long nose and hangdog expression was hardly noticeable.

Back on that evening of 1 November, Noeleen was screaming outside her front door when her neighbour Sam Millward told his wife: 'I think I heard someone out there.' In a quiet place like Coniston Crescent people noticed unusual sounds. Jean Millward dashed out to find Noeleen screaming and sobbing as she crawled up the steps of another neighbour's house.

'Tony, Tony,' Noeleen cried, pointing to her own house.

Neighbours Audrey and John Horrocks opened their door and immediately helped Noeleen into their hallway.

'What's happened,' asked Jean. 'Tell us, dear.'

Noeleen's breathing was uneven. She sobbed: 'There was a... man,' she mumbled. 'Dining room.'

'Come on,' Audrey said to her son Glyn. 'Let's go and see what's happened.'

The front door to the house was wide open as Glyn cautiously led the way in. The hall was in darkness. They could just make out the open patio door, curtains blowing in the wind.

'No one's here, Mum,' announced Glyn.

Then they poked their heads in the lounge and noticed a blanket where Noeleen had been sleeping and the TV was blaring. The only other light in the room came from a gas fire.

The only other light was coming from the upstairs bathroom. Glyn went up followed by his mother. The steps seemed wet and sticky. Then they peered into the main bedroom. 'Go back downstairs, Mum,' Glyn told Jean. 'Don't come up.'

But he was too late. They both stood in the doorway too appalled to say anything at first.

'Quick, call an ambulance,' said Glyn.

Audrey immediately ran back downstairs to the phone. Glyn crept through the semi-darkness to the side of the bed and leaned down to the bloodied figure lying flat on his back.

'You'll be alright, Mr Hendley,' said Glyn. But Tony did not respond.

Glyn went back downstairs and told his mother he had to sit down because he felt faint. It was 11:50pm on November 1, 1991.

The first policeman on the scene was PC Malcolm Kean, who was puzzled when he found the hall light did not work and got a torch from his patrol car. That's when he noticed blood on the carpet, on the walls, even on the furniture in the landing.

In the main bedroom, he found Tony Hendley lying on the bed, his head and shoulders protruding from the bedclothes which were also soaked in blood. The constable tried to lift his head but it was limp. What was the point? He tried to switch on the bedside light and that was when the man he thought was unconscious reached out a hand and touched him.

'Take it easy. An ambulance is coming,' PC Kean told Tony Hendley. 'Can you tell me who did this? What was his name?' All he got was a gargled groan.

Then PC Kean noticed that the man's shirt, soaked in blood, a cardigan and a blood-splattered pair of trousers were all neatly draped on a chair. Even his blood-splattered shoes were neatly positioned under the chair. It seemed as if this man – the victim of a horrendous attack – had managed to put himself to bed after first taking all his clothes off and neatly hanging them over a chair. PC Kean didn't realise that Tony Hendley's army background had instilled discipline in him, whatever the circumstances.

While waiting for the ambulance, PC Kean also noticed a rolling pin covered in blood on the landing. Another policemen who arrived shortly afterwards managed to find a bulb and put it in the landing light socket. That's when he noticed a black balaclava lying on the top stair.

Paramedics eventually arrived and took Tony Hendley to

the Derbyshire Royal Infirmary. After examining his injuries he was then transferred to the neuro-surgical unit at the Queen's Medical Centre in Nottingham, for emergency surgery. The prognosis was not good.

Back in Coniston Cresecent, Noeleen was giving detectives an account of what had happened. She told how her husband had been out with Tony McIntosh, father of their daughter-in-law Kay. Noeleen claimed she had a bad back and had stayed at home to watch TV.

She then said she was about to go to sleep when the car pulled up outside and she heard Tony clanking his way through the wrought-iron side gate. She said he followed his usual routine after a night at the local pub and headed for the toilet for a pee. She even recalled how he's put his head round the door of the lounge on his way up to offer her a cup of tea. She couldn't remember if she'd responded.

She told police how the next thing she heard was 'thump, thump, thump. It sounded like things being knocked over.' Then, said Noeleen, a series of bangs as if he was falling down the stairs. She claimed she rushed into the hallway and called his name but got no response. It was only then she noticed the patio door curtains flapping in the wind. Then a man appeared from nowhere and hit her hard in the face.

Noeleen said she was so badly hurt she fell to the ground and found herself on all fours where she screamed to Tony for help. That's when Tony appeared by the bedroom door unrecognisable after his beating. She told him she'd go and get a neighbour.

'Can I go to Tony, now?' she then asked the detectives.

'Of course, Mrs Hendley. We'll drive you over.'

At the hospital it was a death-watch scenario. Few expected Tony Hendley to live through the night. Noeleen made a point of holding his hand until early Sunday morning when doctors and nurses pronounced no sign of life. They needed her permission to cut off the life support machine. She fought back tears as she nodded and signed the relevant papers. At 9:20am Tony was officially pronounced dead.

The only awkward moment came when it was discovered that Tony had signed an organ donor card. Noeleen wanted his wishes to be honoured but that could have caused enormous problems for the coroner who would now be obliged to carry out a full autopsy. However forensic pathologist Dr Clive Bouch allowed Tony's kidneys to be used for donation because it was clear that his injuries were to the face and head.

Initially, police assumed that it must have been a burglary which had gone badly wrong. In any case, Noeleen couldn't have done it herself because she would have been literally drenched in blood if that had been the case. Blood found on her hands and knees was entirely consistent with her account of crawling up the stairs.

Yet there remained great doubts in the minds of some of the investigating officers. Burglaries in general were very rare in the area where the Hendleys lived and there was the strange matter of that missing light bulb in the hall. The nature of the attack also raised doubts because any one of the 25 blows which rained down on Tony Hendley should have been enough to kill him. Witnesses described his head as looking like a bloody sponge, but why would a burglar hang around battering a man when his main priority was to get away from the scene as quickly as possible?

Even at this early stage, only about half of the detectives involved in the investigation believed it was a genuine burglary. As a result, a unit of policemen decided to concentrate on Tony Hendley's family and friends. In particular they focused on Noeleen Hendley.

Meanwhile Noeleen herself was being photographed in black attending masses in memory of her dead husband and telling the world through the local media about her grief and deep sense of loss.

However, detectives Joe Orrell and Graham Freer, assigned to provide support to the grieving family, soon noticed a different side to Noeleen. There were frequent moments when she seemed cold and distant. And when Noeleen's mother arrived from Dublin she was immediately very hostile to the police.

In January, when the body was finally released for burial, detectives observed the funeral as Noeleen went completely over the top with an outpouring of grief that would have put a Hollywood star to shame. One of the investigators later remarked: 'Something wasn't right. I couldn't put my finger on it.' Even the police were arguing amongst themselves as to whether Noeleen had had her husband killed.

The most obvious clue might have been the life insurance payout. Noeleen got a £69,000 lump sum from Tony's pension scheme at work as well as £285 a month. She was also due two small policies totalling £15,500, but none of this was evidence of her murderous intentions.

Detectives noticed that Noeleen hadn't been to her doctor

to complain about the backache which she claimed had forced her to sleep in the lounge on the night of Tony's murder. Meanwhile another team of detectives, assigned the task of interviewing Derby's lowlife to try and find out the identity of the killer burglar, was having little luck. It was only when police attention turned to a number of slimming clubs run by Noleen that detectives had a lucky break; one woman remembered Noeleen being sent a bunch of red roses at the club. That was all. There was no name attached to the flowers. Maybe it was Tony, but then his friends informed detectives that it just wasn't Tony's style. Eventually the florist who sent the flowers was traced, but she couldn't remember the name of the sender. She was certain, though, that it wasn't Hendley.

Then detectives interviewed one of Noeleen's club members and came away convinced she was lying. The woman was seen four more times by police. But it was only after speaking to her husband that officers discovered the woman had been lying because of her own indiscretions with other men. Now her husband had said he'd forgive his wife so she admitted to officers that Noeleen had been on a date with a man called Terry McIntosh, the father of Noeleen's daughter-in-law.

Noeleen and Terry were immediately hauled into the Cotton Lane police station in Derby and interviewed separately. After six hours of interrogation, Noeleen confessed. When Terry was brought into her interview room, she burst into tears and sobbed, 'I've told them about our affair.'

Terry McIntosh – with his narrow face and balding hairstyle – was a widower whose wife had committed suicide three years earlier. Noeleen later admitted that she saw in him a vulnerable man whom she could manipulate. She tempted him into bed and she was the one who always phoned him to suggest they meet up for sex. They ended up making love in fields, their homes, camper vans, you name it.

Even Noeleen's son Shane wasn't that surprised when the affair was finally made public. He'd even discovered a photo in a drawer at home which he'd only just recognised as his mother. It had been taken on a river boat cruise in London. Noeleen had dropped her trousers and was showing off a rose and butterfly tattoo on her thigh. With the photo was card which read: 'On our anniversary.' The butterfly had been for Terry; the rose signified her allegiance to the rock group Guns N' Roses. Shane handed the photo over to police.

Then investigators stumbled upon the name of 'Bucko' – a supposed hard-man friend of Terry who was reputed to be capable of sorting out any problem. A search of the phone records for the suspects soon revealed that Terry had spent 15 minutes talking to a man called Paul Buxton. When officers called on 40-year-old unemployed electrician Buxton he denied all knowledge of the call but police knew he was holding something back.

Then, the following day, Buxton contacted detectives to say he'd decided to make a full confession after speaking to his family and friends. He'd been haunted by the sight of Tony Hendley dying in front of his eyes. Buxton recalled: 'His eyes were open. I can see his eyes now. Every time I shut my eyes I see his bloody eyes.'

On the afternoon of Tuesday, 28 January, 1992, Paul Buxton was arrested. Noeleen was charged a few hours later and Terry was taken into custody while on a business trip in

Surrey. After an hour of denials about knowing Buxton, Noeleen broke down and admitted her role in the murder and she even told officers about all those earlier failed attempts on her husband's life.

A few months later – in the summer of 1992 – Noeleen admitted to Nottingham Crown Court that her romance with Terry was primarily driven by her insatiable love of sex. She said: 'We had sex as often as possible. I had never experienced such sexual practices before. I couldn't get enough of him. The days never seemed long enough. Terry was like a sex drug. He took me over completely. I just couldn't think for myself any more.' She claimed she thought the plan to kill her husband was all a joke, 'like something out of a film. Things like that don't happen in real life.'

Paul Buxton painted a completely different picture of Noeleen. 'She hated the bloke. I have never seen anybody be married to someone for so long and hate them so much.'

It took the jury less than two-and-a-half hours to convict Noeleen and Paul of murder. Terry had earlier pleaded guilty. All three were given life sentences and Noeleen collapsed in the dock.

Chapter Thirteen:

THE GREEN WIDOW

Cancun, Mexico, is one of those beachside paradises most people can only dream about. Miles and miles of pure golden sand, overlooking the Gulf of Mexico. It is a picturesque, whitewashed town with a handful of luxurious hotels for wealthy American tourists, plus a scattering of bars and restaurants attractively designed to guarantee many thousands of visitors each year.

Mary Ellen Samuels, from Los Angeles, California, had always wanted to travel south of the border. It seemed so exotic on the television – and it appeared to be the perfect place to escape from her worries back in California. So it was, that attractive brunette Mary Ellen found herself on a get-away-from-it-all holiday. The perfect picture was completed by the presence of her young lover, who'd provide the sex and cocaine that had been a staple diet for Mary Ellen throughout her adult life.

Most evenings, she and her handsome lover enjoyed at least two bottles of wine between them in the hotel restaurant before slipping up to their suite where Mary Ellen knew that some athletic lovemaking was sure to occur. One night they'd have sex up against the bedroom door, the next it would be out in the open air on the balcony overlooking the Pacific. And once they were both satisfied, Mary Ellen would unravel herself from him, open a wrap of cocaine and chop out four fat, two-inch lines of white powder. Then she'd pull out a handful of $20 bills, find the crispest note, expertly roll it into a makeshift straw and snort her lines hungrily.

'I got an idea,' her lover said one night, as he snorted the second of his lines. 'Gimme all the cash you got.'

Mary Ellen hesitated for a moment. She'd worked and schemed very hard for her money.

'Come on. I ain't gonna take it. I just wanna show you how to have some fun.'

Mary Ellen threw a holdall on the bed and watched as her boyfriend started spreading $20 bills on top of the bed. Mary Ellen smiled and took a deep, excited breath. Earlier that holiday they'd talked about making love in a sea of the cash; now was the moment to really do it.

Mary Ellen slipped out of her bra and panties and lay on top of the first layer of notes, then her boyfriend carefully covered her body with the crispest of the new $20 bills. Their sharp corners spiked into her flesh, enhancing the sensation of literally swimming in money. Some of the notes dug slightly into her nipples every time she wriggled, while he continued fluttering them all over her.

Eventually, Mary Ellen was totally immersed in the money,

except for a small gap at the top of her thighs. He looked down at her face lying there: she had a smug, satisfied expressed. Then she slowly licked her lips with the tip of her tongue. Her young lover had a broad grin on his face.

'Come on, baby. It's time to show me how much you love me,' exclaimed the sultry former housewife. Her thighs edged apart a few inches. 'Come here.'

The woman dubbed by police as the Green Widow was living up to her name.

Mary Ellen even posed for a photograph, lying naked on that cash. But then that sex romp in a sea of money was just part of her celebration, following a half-a-million dollar insurance payout after the apparently tragic murder of her Hollywood cameraman husband by a cold-blooded stranger.

A few months earlier, the slaying had struck fear into the suburban communities of the San Fernando Valley area of California, just 20 miles from the sprawling metropolis of Los Angeles. Inside the Hollywood movie community, many had mourned the loss of respected technician Bob Samuels, who'd been closely associated with stars like Warren Beatty and Mel Gibson.

Sinking deeper into the mass of green paper, Mary Ellen pulled her young lover on to the bed and proceeded to make hot, passionate love. A luxurious life was, it seemed, hers for the taking. With her neat hairstyle and fondness for sleek, well-fitting power suits, Mary Ellen Samuels looked more like something out of a Dallas soap-opera than a grieving, middle-aged widow. But throughout her marriage she'd nursed a secret addiction to sex, drugs, drink and risk-taking.

For this 45-year-old mother had ordered a hitman to kill

her Hollywood cameraman husband and then murdered that
same hired assassin in case he went to the police. 'It was a
classic story of greed and manipulation combined with a
callous disregard for human life,' prosecuting attorney Jan
Maurizi later said. 'This was a very attractive woman with
short, dark hair who had an uncanny ability to manipulate
people and used her talents to get rich. Just about anybody
whose life she touched became a victim. Basically, her
husband was worth more to Mary Ellen dead than alive.'

This extraordinary story began on 8 December 1988, when
Samuels' husband, 40-year-old Robert B. Samuels – who'd
worked on Hollywood films like *Lethal Weapon* and *Heaven
Can Wait* – was ambushed by an intruder inside the house
the couple had shared until their separation a year earlier.
The 'burglar' shot Samuels in the head with a 16-gauge
shotgun. Police were alerted by Mary Ellen and her 18-year-
old daughter Nicole after they arrived at the house a few
hours later to find her husband's bloodstained corpse. As
Mary Ellen later boasted to friends: 'I should have won an
Academy Award for my acting performance. I was the
perfect, grieving widow.'

But detectives were suspicious about the killing because
there was no apparent sign of a struggle. And it was clear that
Mary Ellen was a very spoiled wife. Within weeks she'd
collected that life insurance payout of $500,000 and went on
a wild spending spree, buying clothes, drugs, cars and holding
parties where couples got naked by the pool.

Mary Ellen splashed out $60,000 on a Porsche, rented
stretch limos most weekends and even took her toyboy to

Mexico on that trip to buy a villa in the sun. As prosecutor Maurizi later explained: 'Mary Ellen was really pretty pampered by her husband. Her child was in private school. I think she had what the average American would consider the good life. But that wasn't good enough for her.' When detectives interviewed Mary Ellen's former husband Ronnie Lee Jamison he told investigators she was a compulsive liar who gambled and used drugs during their marriage.

More than four months after Bob Samuels' murder, detectives established that a hitman had previously failed *three times* to kill Bob Samuels. The hired killer initially plotted with Mary Ellen to push her husband's car off a cliff and twice they'd planned to shoot him after getting him drunk. But each scheme failed at the final hurdle. Eventually, that hitman hired another hitman to finally murder Bob Samuels.

Then, six months after Samuels' slaying, a botany professor on a nature hike found the body of suspected hitman James Bernstein – a 27-year-old reputed cocaine dealer – which had been dumped in a remote canyon in nearby Ventura County. Only later did it emerge that Mary Ellen had hired two more hitmen to do away with Bernstein because he'd started demanding more money and threatened to go to the police if she did not pay. She paid her replacement hitmen just $5,000 and a packet of cocaine to kill Bernstein.

But Mary Ellen Samuels made one stupid mistake. She'd kept original hitman Bernstein's wallet as a souvenir. Police later found it in her Porsche. They also discovered her diary which stated: 'People are saying I did it. Nailed me for Bob, want me for Jim.'

In court, Mary Ellen's defence team tried to claim that Bernstein – who carried a business card calling himself 'James R. Bernstein, specialist' – was smitten with the Samuels' pretty teenage daughter, Nicole. They insisted he acted on his own when he killed Robert Samuels after Nicole told him that Robert Samuels had molested her and raped her when she was just 12 years old. Other friends and relatives of the couple then told the court Mary Ellen had arranged the killing of her husband in revenge for his sex attacks on her daughter. No one was ever able to establish if these claims were true.

Prosecutors dismissed the sexual molestation charges as pure fabrication. And Robert Samuels' sister, Susan Conroy, said, 'It's the ultimate betrayal. He isn't here to defend himself. Bob was a hardworking guy and he loved them very much. He would never have done anything to them.'

Paul Edwin Gaul and Darell Ray Edwards – the men who killed original hitman James Bernstein – testified against Mary Ellen Samuels after striking a deal with prosecutors, who agreed to commute any death sentence against them. They were sentenced before her trial to 15 years to life for the murder of Bernstein.

The court heard that after the Samuels' marriage originally broke up in 1987, Mary Ellen moved out, taking the refrigerator and leaving a five-page 'Dear John' letter. She moved to a condominium in nearby Reseda, California. For more than a year, Mr Samuels hoped they might reconcile. But reconciliation was the furthest thing from Mary Ellen's mind. One old family friend, Heidi Dougall, recalled, 'She hated him and she wanted him done.'

Mary Ellen even told friends that she'd calculated she would only receive $30,000 in a divorce settlement as opposed to the $500,000 she knew her husband was worth dead. Mary Ellen's biggest bone of contention with her husband was over their shared ownership of a sandwich shop in nearby Sherman Oaks. She also didn't want to lose the $1,600 a month in maintenance she was receiving following the separation.

Then, in 1988, Mary Ellen began openly telling friends she was considering having her husband 'done away with'. She even approached some of her daughter's high school friends. Mary Ellen insisted she wanted revenge on her husband because of his alleged attempts to molest her daughter. In one incident at her school, daughter Nicole asked a friend for help as they sat eating in the cafeteria. The stunned classmate later gave courtroom evidence against Mary Ellen.

Mary Ellen Samuels was found guilty of two counts of murder, two counts of conspiracy to murder and two counts of solicitation for murder. 'I've never asked for the death penalty for a woman before,' said prosecutor Maurizi, who was still considering filing charges against her daughter Nicole. 'But these murders were pre-meditated, 6 months apart and motivated purely through greed. Mary Ellen Samuels was a housewife who went shopping for something other suburban housewives don't need. She went shopping for killers!' Prosecutor Maurizi also told the jury: 'I ask you for a verdict of death for all the selfish and inhumane decisions she made in her life. I ask you ladies and gentlemen, how many bodies does it take? We're talking about murder for the sake of the almighty dollar.'

On 16 September 1994, Samuels became only the fifth woman in history to be sentenced to death in California since the state re-imposed capital punishment in the late Seventies. She remains scheduled to die in the gas chamber or through a lethal injection. As juror Karen Hudson explained outside the court following sentencing, 'We wanted to let people know we were sure.'

Chapter Fourteen:

SIZE DOESN'T MATTER

Shelly Molyneux, born in the East End of London the daughter of a maintenance engineer and a seamstress, enjoyed a happy childhood by all accounts. When the family moved to Romford, in Essex, she left school and started work in her local Barclay's Bank. At the age of just 18, she met and fell in love with a customer called Jon Molyneux. The couple were married on 28 June 1980 in the parish church of St Paul's at Bentley Common, in Essex. But not all Shelly's friends and relatives liked her young husband. As her sister Denise later explained: 'I never really warmed to Jon. He could be very condescending towards our family, as if we weren't really good enough for him. Yet Shelly used to say that if they went to a party, he would be the one that everyone wanted to talk to. She really loved and admired him.'

Jon Molyneux was only 5 foot 3 inches tall but he acted

like a *big* man in many other ways, with his pricey Armani suits, Gucci cufflinks and flashy cars. Following their marriage, Shelly gave up work to become a full-time mother and her husband became managing director of Apple Computers UK. Then he struck it really rich during the internet boom as the £175,000-a-year chief executive of Scoot.com.

With all that great wealth came a host of sleazy affairs for pint-sized Jon Molyneux. However, Shelly took the attitude that if she didn't confront her wayward husband then perhaps his adultery might just go away. As her sister later said, 'She would never have contemplated leaving Jon over his affairs because our parents had a long and happy marriage, and she took the view that "we are married and whatever problems we have, we will get over them".'

But not even Shelly could hide her heartbreak when husband Jon left her a couple of times to be with his new girlfriends. 'Sometimes he would ask to come home after a while, saying he'd made a mistake, and other times she would ask him because the children missed their father so much they had begged her to call him.' And every time Jon Molyneux came home he'd buy his wife yet another 'sorry present', such as a piece of jewellery or a brand new car, and they'd try all over again to make a go of their marriage. On Shelly's 40th birthday, husband Jon bought her a Morgan sports car. A few months on – in February 2000 – the couple even renewed their vows at the same church where they were married.

Eleven months later, Jon Molyneux left his wife for a 25-year-old woman called Luisa Bracchi and went to live in west

London. This time, Shelly sued her husband for divorce on grounds of adultery. Later still, Jon was to admit that he'd had over 20 affairs, many of which he'd kept secret from his wife.

Then, in August 2001, Shelly met divorced father-of-one Paul McGuinness, who was more than ten years her junior. She soon told Paul all about her marriage problems. As he later explained: 'I was aware of the problems she was having with Jon, but she used to say, "I don't want to get you involved in all that."'

However, relations between Shelly and her ex-husband grew steadily more acrimonious. One day she got an email from Jon accusing her of being 'a leech'. Another message described her as being a 'manipulative witch'. It got so bad that Shelly made sure she was out whenever her ex-husband came to visit their children, and by Christmas of 2001 the couple only communicated through solicitors. Then Jon's career took a bit of a nosedive and he announced to his wife that their two children would have to be taken out of private schools. Her sister Denise later explained: 'She was at absolute rock bottom and Jon had rescinded on a deal over the house and she didn't know where she was going to live with the children.'

Shelly became convinced that her ex-husband had more money than he was admitting, so in February 2002, she hired a private investigator called Gavin Burrows to check out Jon Molyneux's finances. His name had initially been spotted and then suggested by Shelly's young love, Paul McGuinness. Burrows had advertised in the back of a legal magazine and McGuinness knew a solicitor who'd used the private eye a couple of times. Shelly paid him £3,000 to launch a proper investigation of her ex-husband's finances.

It wasn't long before Burrows rang her to say he'd traced an account containing £83,000 in Jon's name to Bermuda. And at the same time she told the private eye how badly her former husband was treating her.

Then one day the conversation took a more sinister turn. As Shelly's lover Paul McGuinness later explained: 'When she said she wanted him out of her life, the conversation turned to finding a permanent solution.' Without telling her lover, Shelly Molyneux agreed to meet a hitman, recommended to her by Gavin Burrows, two days before she and her lover were due to go on a skiing holiday together in February 2002. In a videotape recording of that conversation later revealed in court, Shelly clearly stated that she 'wished to take the matter further'. What she didn't realise was that the 'hitman' was an undercover tabloid reporter, who later went to the police.

Over the kitchen table of the family home, Shelly Molyneux told the supposed hitman: 'I've spent 20 years with a man who has been an absolute bastard. He's been making my life hell. He wants to destroy me. I will not let him keep doing this to me. I hate him. I want him gone forever. He's an easy target, I would think, being 5 foot 3. And he's flash. He wears Armani suits and he drives an Audi. I am looking at a hijacking. I am looking at a mugging.' But Shelly Molyneux wasn't finished yet. She added, 'I've wished him a heart attack or said I hoped to stress him out so much he would have a stroke. I told him, "I hope you burn in hell," but those were just normal divorce things.'

Then the hitman asked her on the tape how long she'd been thinking about having her husband killed and she replied, 'A year.' Then she was asked if she was sure. 'Very sure.' And she added, 'I was a normal wife and mother until all this happened. But please be very, very careful. This is the rest of my life we're talking about and I want my children to have their mother around.' Shelly claimed the hitman then said he would call her later that night to confirm she wanted him to go ahead and kill her ex-husband. She went on to say that when he didn't call she assumed the hit had been cancelled. (Shelly Molyneux's lover, Paul McGuinness, later described watching the videotape as 'like watching a complete stranger. When she is under intense pressure, she tends to put on an act and comes across as flippant and blasé, while inside she is in a state of trauma.')

Then, on that skiing holiday in Canada, Shelly got two phone calls which so frightened her, she later claimed, that she put a block on her mobile phone because she thought that because she hadn't given any money to the hitman he wouldn't go ahead and murder Jon Molyneux. One of those calls was actually from a policeman posing as another hitman. A court later heard that he'd offered her the opportunity to back down but she did not take it.

The first Paul McGuinness knew of his lover's bid to kill her ex-husband was when the pair returned from Canada with three of her children and were stopped at customs by police at Gatwick Airport and taken to separate interview rooms. As McGuinness later recalled, 'After three hours they took her to a central London police station and I had to find her children in the airport. When I told them, they became completely hysterical.'

McGuinness then took Shelly's children to their

grandparents' home in Essex. It wasn't until two days later that McGuinness was allowed to see his lover at the police station where she was being held. 'It was very emotional,' he later recalled. 'Shelly was terrified I might leave her, and the children would have no one to look after them.'

Shelly Molyneux insisted to her lover she had no intention of meeting the hitman and that the private eye had insisted she go ahead with the meeting. 'She was terrified that, if she didn't meet him, the family might come to harm,' McGuinness later said. After ten days on remand in Holloway Prison, Shelly was freed on bail and Paul McGuinness proposed marriage to her in August 2002.

In October, 2002, Shelly Molyneux was jailed for five years after admitting soliciting for murder. Judge Christopher Moss said Molyneux was 'motivated by greed and hatred' and was 'deadly serious' in wanting her husband murdered. At her trial she'd been dubbed 'evil', 'cold-blooded' and 'greedy' – a woman who would stop at nothing to inherit a fortune of more than £1 million in cash and a £600,000 insurance policy. She later insisted to her family that she never really wanted her former husband dead but was lured into the plot by a private investigator who saw a chance to make money from a tabloid newspaper. Even Jon Molyneux had asked the court to be lenient on his wife for the sake of their children.

'Shelly is full of regret. I do not believe she ever really wanted Jon dead,' says Paul McGuinness. 'When she hired Gavin Burrows [the private investigator] she was on the verge of a nervous breakdown. She was out of her mind with worry over what would happen to her and the children. She didn't want Jon's money, she just wanted the house. The insurance policy she was supposed to be after had already been signed over to the children and his new partner.

'This whole murder plot was simply a fantasy that spun out of control. She was at rock bottom, terrified she would lose the family home, and simply had the misfortune to voice those feelings to Gavin Burrows. When it all got out of hand she was too terrified to tell them to stop in case they harmed her children. She thought if she simply refused to take their calls or hand over any money, the murder wouldn't go ahead.'

Nothing could soften the blow of that five-year sentence for Shelly Molyneux. Her children refused to have anything more to do with their father and now they look forward to her regular letters from prison and the three phone calls she is allowed to make each week. Four times a month they make the one-and-a-half-hour journey to High Point Prison in Suffolk to visit their mother.

In the five or ten minutes she is permitted, she asks them in turn how they are coping without her and if they still love her. Then she turns to lover Paul McGuinness, who is now caring for the children aged 18, 17, 15 and 6, telling him how lonely and frightened she is.

Shelly Molyneux is planning an appeal against her sentence. If she fails, it will be another two years at the earliest before she will be considered for parole. Some consider Shelly was at best foolish in the extreme and at worst downright murderous.

Chapter Fifteen:

RING RING

The shrill of a bell ringing loudly in the distance meant only one thing to Judy Benkowski – her husband was demanding something. Clarence Benkowski was overweight and overbearing. All his life he'd been number one in that miserable household. And even now, after retiring from his job as a welder, he expected to be waited on hand and foot.

When his sick and aged mother decided to move in it got worse for Judy, because it meant there were two of them bullying and cursing her. They made her serve them as if she was a slave. They treated her like dirt. There had to be a better way to spend your life, surely?

Often these two obese specimens would sit in their cosy armchairs in the sitting room of the Benkowski's neat, detached suburban home at number 508, South Yale Avenue, Addison, near Chicago, for hours on end without lifting a finger. That was when the wretched little bell rang the most.

An endless stream of demands followed.

Ring. 'Get me a coffee,' said one.

Ring. 'Get me a beer,' said the other.

Ring. 'This coffee's cold, get me another.'

Ring. 'This beer's not cold enough. Why the hell aren't they kept in the freezer?'

And so it went. On and on and on. Judy Benkowski had no time for a job and only a small handful of friends in the entire world. Her main occupation was looking after those two leeches, as well as bringing up her two sons.

Not surprisingly, it sometimes got too much for Judy. Her life was so relentless and so unenjoyable that she'd often cry herself to sleep at night, wondering when it would ever end. Occasionally, husband Clarence would drunkenly try to have sex with her. It certainly wasn't making love. Judy reckoned it was closer to rape than anything else.

The act of sex was totally one-sided. He'd make her fondle him and then – at the very moment he was ready – she would just lie there and listen to him grunting while his blubbery, obese body crushed her into the mattress. At such moments, she'd try and think of other things, like the next day's shopping. But his roughness would snap her back to the unpleasant reality of having this huge lump of lard molesting her. But at least it was usually over in minutes, if not seconds. However the pain could be really awful sometimes. Pretty inevitable when a seriously overweight middle-aged man forces himself on a slightly built, five-foot-tall woman more than 20 years his junior. They might have been husband and wife in law. But they were complete strangers in every other sense of the word.

One day Clarence decided he wanted to spice up *his* sex life so he bought a waterbed. Typically, it was the cheapest one he could find and it had the unpleasant side-effect of being so under-filled that it swayed from side to side and made its occupants feel seasick. So instead of just lying there, now Judy had that awful, overwhelming sensation of rocking up and down on a boat bobbing across the ocean. Often she'd almost gag as the bile tried to force its way out of her throat. At least then her husband would stop forcing himself into her rather than risk being puked over.

Clarence's attitude towards sex was much the same as his outlook on life: men ruled the household. Women were just there to honour and obey and do what the hell he said. He didn't give a damn about Judy's feelings, he just wanted four big, square meals a day and an orgasm when he felt like it.

For almost 20 years, Judy put up with the insults and misery of married life. What else could she do? She had no career. She couldn't afford to exist outside those four walls. She'd been trapped for so long she'd forgotten what it was like to enjoy herself.

'You cannot let him treat you like this. You gotta do somethin' about it, Judy.'

Debra Santana was outraged by her friend Judy Benkowski's complete indifference to her appalling marital situation. She'd heard so many horror stories from Judy. How could a husband treat his wife so badly? Debra assured her friend she certainly wouldn't put up with it.

'But,' Judy explained, in her quiet, reserved way, 'what can I do? I have nowhere to go. No means of support.'

However, Debra was determined to help her friend and neighbour. They had an unlikely kinship. Debra was a striking blonde of 32, with a fun-loving attitude towards life, who'd suffered during her marriage and taken the sensible route out: divorce. She now enjoyed everything that Judy had long since given up hope of having.

The main object of envy between the two women was Debra's athletic, black lover who, she regularly told Judy, gave her all-round sexual satisfaction and never treated her badly. Judy was envious because all she really wanted was to feel warmth, passion and true love again from a man. Judy knew Debra was right when she said she had to do something about her marriage, but what?

Judy's husband Clarence, a strict Catholic, wouldn't even discuss the subject of divorce. And he wasn't prepared to let them lead separate lives. At least then she could have gone out with other men and he could have done as he pleased. But Clarence believed he owned Judy – lock, stock and barrel. She was his woman. If he wanted sex he'd ring his bell and get it. If he wanted to insult her he'd do it. If he wanted her to be his slave nothing could stop him, or so he told Judy with great relish virtually every day of their miserable marriage.

Judy's friend Debra continued to be outraged. She may have been 13 years younger than her friend, but she gradually achieved increasing influence over her weaker neighbour. The more they talked about Debra's adventures in and out of bed, the more Judy began to realise how desperate she was to end the misery.

'But what can I do about him?' Judy asked her friend one day.

'I've got an idea …' replied Debra.

Eddie Brown was the lover who'd given Debra all the sexual satisfaction she'd ever craved. Even fully clothed, Eddie's muscular, toned torso virtually burst his shirt buttons to breaking point. Judy Benkowski felt a tingle of excitement as she shook his hand for the first time. She didn't need much imagination to work out what Eddie's biggest asset must have been.

'Eddie's going to help you with your problem, Judy,' said Debra, when all three met up one day in a local restaurant.

The only thing about Eddie that did surprise Judy was that he stood just 5 foot 3 inches tall. In fact, Debra towered over him by at least three inches. But none of that mattered because Debra had convinced Judy that Eddie was going to be the perfect man to help cure her marriage problems. But it was a job that required a certain amount of planning.

'D'you really think you can kill him without being caught?' Judy asked Eddie Brown.

He assured both women he could murder Judy's husband Clarence with 'no trouble'. He even agreed a fee of $5,000 as they sat round that table in the restaurant.

Admittedly, there were a few details to sort out. Where should it be done? What weapon should be used? How would they make sure the police didn't suspect anything? And what happened if he lived?

At first, Judy Benkowski wondered if she'd gone completely crazy. How could she even contemplate murdering another human being? It all seemed like a dream. She hesitated.

'Maybe we shouldn't do this,' she told her best friend and the woman's lover.

There was a brief silence from Debra and Eddie.

'What?' said Debra. 'You can't change your mind. We agreed on this, Judy. Come on. Let's do it!'

Then Eddie chipped in, 'Yeah. It'll be easy. We'll make it look like a robbery. No problem.'

The pressure was mounting on Judy. She wasn't a strong-willed woman at the best of times. Now she felt as if there really wasn't any choice in the matter. After all, this was her only real escape route from a miserable life. It was the answer to all her problems and unhappiness. Sure it seemed drastic, but that animal of a husband deserved to die. He'd treated her like dirt for too long. Now it was her turn. Revenge would be sweet. There was no turning back.

Next they had to decide how and where to do it.

It was mid-October 1988, and Halloween was fast approaching. Judy had a great idea, which she immediately enthusiastically shared with her two partners in crime.

'I'll get you [Eddie] a real scary costume. You'll look just like a kid out trick-or-treating. Then you knock on the door, Clarence answers. You scream "trick or treat" and he gets shot to death. Whaddya think?'

Debra and Eddie looked stunned. It was a ludicrous plan and they knew it. But Judy had come to life describing the ghoulish aspects of it. She'd even chuckled weirdly as she described the shooting of her husband. And she wasn't finished yet.

'Clarence is a mean son-of-a-bitch and he hates giving anything to people who come knocking at the door. I kinda like the idea of him getting the ultimate payback.'

The shy, retiring Judy Benkowski had been suddenly transformed into a hard-nosed killer psyching herself up for murder. Her sudden obsession with husband Clarence's death even surprised her great friend Debra. But Judy felt that the risks involved were far outweighed by the prospect of a new life without Clarence. Judy Benkowski was feeling happier than she had done for years.

'But hang on there, Judy,' said Eddie. 'Trick-or-treaters don't usually gun down their neighbours. The cops would suss it was a contract hit and they'd get us for sure.'

Pint-sized Eddie was trying to defuse the situation. Sure, he'd agreed to murder this lady's husband because the guy sounded like he deserved it. But Judy's scheme was absolutely insane. It was like something out of a comic book, hardly the sort of low-key killing Eddie had in mind. He'd just got out of jail and was hoping to avoid any future spells in the slammer.

'I think we gotta do something less ...' he hesitated,' ... dramatic?'

Judy was shaking her head before he'd even finished saying it.

'No way. The cops'll think some crazy trick-or-treater is out there blasting innocent citizens to death. They'll never think it was a contract killing.'

Debra and Eddie glanced at each other and shrugged their shoulders. All they could see were the dollar signs registering in front of their eyes.

'You're the boss,' said Eddie. He was jobless and needed the money so he wasn't about to blow the contract, whatever the risks.

Halloween trick-or-treating involves children dressed in ghoulish costumes knocking on their neighbours' doors and shouting 'trick or treat' when someone opens up. The traditional reward is a liberal helping of sweets and, usually, everyone goes home happy. In the Chicago suburb of Addison – as in tens of millions of homes across the United States – these Halloween activities had been fervently obeyed ever since a group of devil worshippers in Salem started the ball rolling more than 200 years earlier. And South Yale Avenue – where the Benkowskis lived – was no exception. With its row upon row of three-bedroomed detached bungalows, built to maximise the use of space available, this was classic Middle-American suburbia.

But on Halloween afternoon, small-time crook Eddie Brown started to get cold feet. As Judy and Debra adjusted the ghoulish latex face mask they'd bought him at the local supermarket, Eddie felt that dressing up like a kid going out trick-or-treating was not the right way to go about a professional hit.

To make matters worse, the rubbery mask was extremely hot, sweaty and tight fitting. Judy and Debra had insisted on getting one that covered his entire face so that no one could see what colour his skin was. But it was airless behind that mask. Eddie started wondering if he'd even make it to number 508 alive. Gasping for air, he complained to the two women, 'This is fuckin' crazy. I can't even see properly outta the eye slits.'

Eddie's voice was so badly muffled by the mask, the two women didn't understand what he was saying at first.

So he yelled, 'I SAID, "THIS IS CRAZY."'

If Eddie had to shout this loudly to be heard, then he'd probably alert the entire street when he went knocking on Clarence Benkowski's door to announce his trick-or-treating surprise. But yet more problems lay ahead.

When Eddie wandered up the street to the end of South Yale Avenue his heart sank. Dozens of school children were marching up and down the street in trick-or-treating disguises. It looked as if the entire population of under-15-year-olds in Addison had all decided to hit South Yale at exactly the same time.

Eddie ripped off the mask in a fit of frustration and stood there in his white skeleton costume, jumping up and down on the spot. His two female accomplices looked at him with horror.

'I'm not doin' this. I can't start shootin' at the guy in front of all those kids. I'll never get away with it.'

Eddie abandoned the hit there and then. Judy was furious. She'd been dreaming about that ugly hulk of a husband being gunned down. Now Eddie Brown was ruining all her plans.

'But you gotta do it, Eddie. You cut a deal.'

But Eddie Brown had a new plan in mind.

'Don't get me wrong, Judy. I'll kill that son-of-a-bitch. But not tonight. It'd be crazy and we'd all end up in jail.'

Judy reluctantly agreed.

'OK. But it's gotta be soon.'

Ring. 'Where's my breakfast?'

Ring. 'Come on, I'm goddam hungry.'

Ring. Ring. Ring.

Clarence Benkowski was providing his usual pre-breakfast performance. At least on this day his mother was away at a relative's, so Judy didn't have to put up with her as well. In the kitchen, Judy muttered quietly under her breath, *'Don't worry. You'll get just what you deserve in good time.'*

If Clarence hadn't been so lazy, he might have got up from the breakfast table where he was slouched and lumbered into the kitchen to witness Judy pouring the contents of twenty sachets of sleeping pills into his coffee.

Instead he just kept on ringing that damn bell.

Ring. 'Move your ass, woman. I'm HUNGRY.'

That last ring was the signal which would hopefully mark the beginning of the end of Clarence Benkowski's life. For it helped Judy feel no guilt as she emptied the last of those packets and then swilled them around in his coffee. The more he rang the bell, the better she felt about killing him. It was a wonderful feeling – just to contemplate the end of her unhappy life.

Just keep ringing, Clarence. Just keep ringing. Soon you'll never ring again.

Then Judy tipped the empty pill packets into the trashcan, before moving towards the dining area with a new spring in her step, a new bounce in her walk.

'There you go, sweetheart.'

She hadn't called him that for years. 'Sweetheart' was a term of endearment. How could she have even contemplated feeling warmth towards this lazy, fat bully of a man she was about to murder. Yet a tingle of excitement and passion ran through Judy's body as she put the tray down on the breakfast table. Then she sat down and quietly sipped at her tea, her eyes straining upwards and across the table towards Clarence. But he hadn't even lifted the coffee cup yet.

Clarence Benkowski was a predictable creature of habit. He liked to first gulp down his fried eggs, then stuff some crunchy toast into that big fat mouth of his. Then that cup of coffee would be lifted to his lips. *Be patient. Relax. He's going to drink it. All in good time. All in good time.*

The *Chicago-Sun Times* was spread across the table in front of Clarence, as it always was each morning. Something caught his eye. He stopped eating and gaped at the sports results.

Not once in all their years together had he even uttered a word of conversation to Judy over breakfast. That was another of his most cherished habits. But that cup of coffee remained untouched. Judy's initial excitement was starting to slide into desperation. *Come on! Come on! Get on with it!*

She felt desperate. Maybe it was time for desperate measures.

'Sweetheart.' For some weird reason she used *that* word again. 'Sweetheart, drink your coffee or it'll get cold.'

For a few seconds, Clarence screwed up his blubbery face and looked at his wife quizzically. She *never* spoke at breakfast. Why the hell was she bugging him to drink his coffee? Never before in more than 20 years. Why now? But, as with most things in Clarence's life, he gave it no more than a brief moment of consideration. Any further analysis would have been totally out of character.

Judy was angry with herself for weakening in the face of such adversity. She mustn't try to make him drink his coffee or he might get suspicious. She didn't dare look up again in case he caught her eye and saw those telltale signs of guilt.

Judy was virtually shaking with anxiety. Maybe she'd

blown it. Had he sussed her out? She shut her eyes for a split second in the hope all that doubt and anguish would simply go away.

Then it happened. The unmistakable slurping noise was like music to her ears. She opened her eyes to see him gulping like a fat bull at a water trough as he tried to wash all that greasy food down his big, ugly gullet. At last, he was going to pay the ultimate price for his cruelty and greed.

As he sucked that big coffee cup dry, Judy felt the rush of relief running through her veins. She sighed quietly to herself. She later admitted it was one of the most satisfying moments of her life.

Seconds later ...

'I don't feel so good. Think I'll lie down a while,' belched Clarence.

The sleeping pills were already kicking in.

The previous day, pint-sized Romeo, Eddie Brown had provided Judy with very precise instructions on how many tablets she should feed him. Just enough to knock him into a deep slumber rather than complete unconsciousness. That way, no one would be able to tell he'd been drugged.

Clarence Benkowski got up and struggled towards the bedroom. He only just managed to get to his beloved waterbed before collapsing in a heap of rolling fat. A few seconds later, Judy crept into the room just to make sure he was out. Then she walked quietly back into the hallway and phoned Debra. 'He's asleep. You and Eddie better get over here fast.'

Judy put the phone down gently and awaited her two accomplices.

Debra was the first to turn up at the house. She hugged Judy warmly to show her good friend she supported her completely and utterly. The two women then walked into the front room and sat side by side on a sofa and counted the minutes until Eddie arrived. Eventually the back door opened with a creak and their hired killer walked in.

In almost complete silence, Judy handed Eddie her husband's World War Two Luger pistol and motioned him towards the master bedroom where the master lay sleeping on his waterbed.

The two women then sat back down on the same sofa. Debra put on a pair of stereo headphones and began listening to heavy metal on her Walkman. She didn't want to hear what was about to occur.

Eddie had earlier said he'd use a pillow to muffle the sound of the gun, but that didn't prevent Judy from hearing the thudding pops of three bullets being fired into her husband's slumbering torso. She didn't feel any great outpouring of emotion. Just a sense of relief that it was finally over.

But there was more work still to be done. Judy and her two accomplices needed to make it look like a burglary that had gone wrong. All three began pulling drawers of clothes out and spread them all over the bed where Clarence still lay. Incredibly, the waterbed was still intact because all three bullets had embedded themselves in their target. Judy was disappointed in a way because she really hated that waterbed. But then it would have caused such a mess if it'd leaked everywhere.

Meanwhile, Eddie continued smashing the place to bits so as to make it look like the house had been robbed. But all this was proving much more stressful to Judy than the murder of her husband.

'No. Not the china, please,' she begged him.

Judy stopped Eddie destroying her vast collection of china memorabilia which she'd lovingly collected for many years. Eddie was irritated.

'This is supposed to look like a robbery.'

'Surely, we can still make it look good without wrecking my china?'

Eddie shrugged his shoulders. Judy was paying him, so it was her decision.

Before Eddie was to flee out of the back door, Judy had to hand over the first instalment of $1,000. She also allowed Eddie to take two rings from a jewellery drawer as a 'bonus'. The rest of the cash would be given to him within a week. Seconds later Eddie had disappeared. Mission accomplished.

After he'd gone, the two women embraced. They'd done it. They'd got rid of the animal. Now there was a big wide world out there waiting to be conquered. It was going to be the beginning of Judy Benkowski's new life. But before they could leave the ransacked house, Judy checked down the street. It was mid-morning; husbands were at work, mothers were out shopping. Not a person in sight. They strolled casually out into the bright autumn sunlight.

The Italian restaurant where Judy and Debra went to celebrate that lunchtime was so crowded that the only thing noticeable about them was that they ordered a bottle of very expensive white wine. Few citizens in Middle America drink alcohol at lunchtime so their toast to one another raised a few eyebrows.

'To us. Long may we live without husbands.' They chuckled before downing each glass in virtually one gulp. And it wasn't just a new life of freedom that Judy was looking forward to; Clarence's life insurance was worth at least $100,000 and then there was the $150,000 resale value of the family house.

Judy Benkowski reckoned she was going to be a very merry widow indeed.

'He's been murdered. He's been murdered.'

Judy's hysterical voice sounded very convincing to local police detective sergeant Tom Gorniak. He'd been patched through to the Benkowski home after Addison police station had received an emergency call from Debra and Judy, who'd just 'discovered' Clarence Benkowski shot dead on their return from a 'shopping trip'.

In a bizarre three-way conference call between the detective's radio, the police station switchboard and Judy Benkowski, DS Gorniak tried to ascertain what had happened as he drove at high speed to South Yale Avenue to answer their emergency call. By the time he rolled up at the house, paramedics had already arrived. Gorniak found the two women weeping in the front yard, tried to console them and then got a uniformed officer to keep an eye on them while he carefully examined the crime scene before the police technicians arrived. Gorniak knew this was the best time to look around because everything remained untouched and exactly as it had been at the time of the murder. He was immediately puzzled by the way in which the victim's body lay slumped in bed as if he'd been taking an afternoon nap. How could he have slept through the noise of an intruder who then leaned over him and fired three bullets into his head at close range?

Burglars just didn't usually do that sort of thing. Even in trigger-happy America burglars rarely used their weapons. Most professional burglars would get the hell out of a house the moment they were disturbed. So Gorniak quickly concluded that the victim was asleep when he was shot. He didn't even have time to turn around and see his killer.

Then investigator Gorniak noticed the clothes thrown from the drawers over the body. That meant the killer had ransacked the room *after* the shooting. It just didn't make sense. He wouldn't have bothered to do that, surely?

Tom Gorniak had been a policeman for ten years and he knew only too well how dangerous it was to draw any conclusions at such an early stage in a murder investigation. But he was convinced this looked like a contract killing.

Outside, he leaned into the squad car where Judy was sitting and asked her, 'Did your husband have any enemies, Mrs Benkowski?'

Gorniak tried to be gentle. After all, this was the grieving widow he was talking to, and she seemed to be really upset.

'No,' Judy replied through sniffs. 'He had no enemies.'

But Tom Gorniak had a hunch, so he persuaded Judy Benkowski to visit the police station with him that evening. He said he knew how bad she must be feeling, but it was important they went through a few details so that the killer could be quickly apprehended. Judy agreed. She didn't want to seem to be hindering the police enquiries in any way. Soon Gorniak and his colleague Detective Mike Tierney were gently probing the widow for clues. They were already convinced she had a lot more to tell them about this case.

Naturally, Judy started getting a little edgy. She had to tell them something so maybe a half-truth would keep them happy.

'Now I remember, I did notice someone outside the house this morning,' she recalled anxiously to the two detectives.

Gorniak and Tierney raised their eyebrows. Why didn't she mention this before?

Judy then described in precise detail how she'd returned from her shopping trip with her friend Debra and they'd seen this rather short, stocky black man.

'I think he was runnin' away from the house,' explained Judy.

The two officers were even more puzzled. They began pulling in the reins. Both sensed that Judy Benkowski knew a lot more than she was admitting. Their next move was to haul Judy's friend Debra Santana in for questioning. As the detectives waited with Judy for Debra to arrive, they tried an old and trusted police technique.

'It would sure help us if you could tell us everything you know. How about we start from the beginning again,' asked Tom Gorniak.

Judy hesitated. She had a lot on her mind and she was starting to think that maybe the officers were well aware of it. Then she took a long, deep breath. 'Well, I think I knew that black guy running away from my house. His name is Eddie Brown. He's Debra's boyfriend.'

Tom Gorniak and Mike Tierney looked at each other and smiled. They knew they were about to hear a confession to murder. As Gorniak later explained: 'After all that planning, Judy Benkowski went and gave it all away before her husband's body was virtually cold.'

In September 1989, Judy Benkowski sobbed uncontrollably as she was sentenced to 100 years in prison for hiring hitman Eddie Brown to murder her husband. Du Page County prosecutor Michael Fleming had earlier demanded that Judy get the death penalty, but Judge Brian Telander ruled that there were mitigating factors that 'precluded the imposition of the death penalty'.

These included no prior criminal record, numerous health problems and several character witnesses who testified on her behalf and told the court her husband was a lazy bully of a man. Prosecutor Fleming described the sentence – which meant Judy would not be eligible for parole until she was 97 – as 'fair and appropriate. She claimed she wanted a divorce and he wouldn't go along, but she never even talked to a lawyer about it.'

On 31 August 1991, Judy married sweetheart Clarence Jeske at the Dwight Correctional Institute, in Illinois. The couple had first met before her husband was murdered but they both insist their relationship did not begin until after the killing. By a strange twist of fate, Jeske now lives in that same house where Clarence was murdered, in South Yale Avenue. He's even been made legal guardian of Judy's two children.

Chapter Sixteen:

EMERGENCY LANDING

The noise of aircraft taking off from nearby Heathrow Airport every 30 seconds is the sound that dominates life in Hounslow, Middlesex, a sprawling concrete jungle of high-rise estates and tatty between-the-wars housing. Not surprisingly, property prices have remained low in Hounslow. It's stuck in a no-man's-land between the city and the countryside but in recent years has become a magnet for Asian immigrants.

These hard-working people have opened numerous shops and businesses and live the sort of lifestyles many of them could never have achieved back in their homeland. And without those many hundreds of thousands of immigrants from countries like India and Pakistan, corner shops in the UK might have become a thing of the past, as the huge supermarket chains continue to swallow up customers at an alarming rate. In Hounslow, many of these small businesses stay open virtually all day and night providing their owners with healthy profits.

The other reason why the Asian population in places like Hounslow has done such good business is that many shops are staffed by members of their own family. Wives, sons, daughters, mothers and fathers are expected to do their fair share behind the counter and many are already living on the premises. It certainly saves them a packet in wages.

Mohinder Cheema was one such classic example of a successful Asian businessman in Hounslow. Since arriving in Britain in the Fifties, he'd gradually bought up an off-licence, two shops and numerous other residential properties at a time when prices were but a fraction of what they are today. But he liked to keep his success close to his chest. Even his attractive dark-haired wife, Julie, didn't know exactly how much Mohinder Cheema was worth, even though they'd been married for many years and had brought up three children.

There were times when 44-year-old Julie Cheema wondered why she'd married her husband in the first place because they seemed to have so little in common. Their romance and eventual wedding in 1985 had surprised both their families. He was the frail, yet astute millionaire. She came from a traditional British background.

Julie later admitted she was attracted to Mohinder's business acumen. He had a wonderful eye for a deal; an ability to make money out of nothing. She had seen him as 'a good investment'. But that kind of attitude is not usually enough to keep a marriage intact. For there was another side to her husband that most women would find hard to cope with. Mohinder Cheema suffered from chronic asthma and frequently had to retire to bed when his breathing became seriously affected. As a result, the couple rarely had sex together after their children were born.

Initially, Julie had been a very sympathetic nurse to her husband, but she gradually began to resent the constant interruptions to her life. And she longed for some passion in their marriage. So Julie Cheema started looking elsewhere for affection.

Neil Marklew was a gangly youth of just 19 when he first met Julie Cheema. He lived with his parents in Catherine Gardens, just around the corner from the Cheemas' main off-licence in Cromwell Road, Hounslow. Initially, Marklew didn't even notice Julie's hand brush his as she gave him change in the shop. He certainly didn't realise she fancied him. Julie Cheema felt lonely and rejected at this time. Her husband was becoming more and more short-tempered as his asthma attacks become increasingly regular and they rarely even slept in the same bed. At first, this unlikely twosome became genuine friends and there was no relationship between them. But despite a 25-year age difference, Neil and Julie found they had a lot in common.

Then Mohinder Cheema started threatening to cut his wife out of his will. He accused Julie of not being truly in love with him. Mohinder's children from an earlier marriage disliked Julie and they warned their father not to trust her. Mohinder then started to question his wife's reasons for marrying him in the first place. Had she been after his wealth all along?

The relationship between Julie and her husband had reached an all-time low by the summer of 1990. Life at home had become one long round of arguments and tension. Mohinder Cheema spent even more of his time in bed and his wife was trying to stay out of the house whenever possible. Then Julie arrived home early one evening and was about to enter her husband's bedroom when she heard voices. It was one of Mohinder's grown-up sons. She stopped in her tracks and waited and listened. The voices were loud and clear. They were discussing Mohinder's will and how Julie was going to be cut out of it. She waited a few moments longer and then silently tiptoed away. She didn't want them to know she'd been listening because she had a plan that none of them should know about.

Neil Marklew's relationship with Julie Cheema soon developed into something special. They'd meet in the middle of the day while her husband was working in the shop or lying in bed sick. Neil – who was unemployed – enjoyed their chats together because it broke up the monotony of life on the dole. The days were the most boring time of all for him because most of his friends were either at college or out working.

During the hot summer of 1990, the couple met in parks, pubs and coffee shops to talk about life, love and Mohinder Cheema. Julie became increasingly obsessed with her husband's plans to cut her out of the will. She also knew that her husband was watching her every move and suspected she was getting some physical gratification from elsewhere. In fact, Julie had not committed adultery – yet. She was content having a companion to confide in, even if he was young enough to be her son.

But teenager Neil Marklew's affection for Julie was growing by the day. He started thinking about her virtually every waking moment. The more they met and talked, the more he began to want to have a proper affair with her. Up until then, they'd done nothing more than kiss on street corners and stroke hands over the tops of coffee-shop tables. Virtually no one knew about their secret liaisons. Neil believed his mates would rib him mercilessly if they found out, and Julie certainly had no intention of telling a living soul. Neil was prepared to do anything to encourage turning their friendship into the real thing.

'I'd kill him for you if you asked me,' he told her one day.

Neil Marklew later claimed he'd wanted to show Julie how much he cared for her. But she took it literally.

'Do you mean that?'

The teenager hesitated for a moment and looked into Julie Cheema's eyes. He desperately wanted to have her completely to himself.

'Sure I do,' he mumbled. She didn't even notice his reserved response.

'I hate him, you know,' said Julie. 'I've been thinking of killing him for ages but I don't know how.'

Neil Marklew had opened up a can of worms over which he had little control. Now he was discovering what it would take to win Julie's love forever. He sat there nodding his head as she continued.

'There must be a way we could do it.'

That's when it dawned on Neil that this might be a way out of the doldrums of unemployment. Of course he was in love with her but there were *other* considerations.

'Well, it'll cost you.'

'How much do you think?'

'You tell me – what's he worth?'

'Five million.'

Neil let out a long whistle. He had no idea his sweetheart's husband was worth that sort of money.

'I'd just be happy to have the off-licence.'

'OK. It's yours if you do the job properly,' replied Julie.

The truth was that Julie Cheema had a highly inflated opinion of her husband's real wealth. But one off-licence seemed a small price to pay for the £5 million she believed her husband was worth in total. In reality it was about one-fifth of that sum.

'Right, give me some money and I'll get a gun,' said Neil, who was starting to enjoy his role as the fixer. Then he told her he knew just the bloke for the job of hitman.

Robert Naughton, aged 20, was even more desperate for money than his friend Neil Marklew. He was unemployed but didn't even have the luxury of his parents' handouts to fall back on. So when Marklew suggest there might be a 'little job' on the horizon he was all ears. When Marklew passed Naughton a sawn-off shotgun and told him the victim was to be his girlfriend's husband, he didn't bat an eyelid. The two friends finished off their pints of bitter in a local tavern and walked out to prepare for the job they hoped would set them up with a business for life.

'Bang. Bang.' Neil turned to his pal. 'It'll be as easy as that.'

It was a steaming hot day in Hounslow in August 1990. Business in cold drinks was brisk at the Cheemas' off-licence in Cromwell Road and Mohinder Cheema must have been hoping the good weather would continue. He and his wife were both in the shop during the late afternoon that day. Julie was giving the place a good clean and her husband was sitting – due to his bad health – behind the counter waiting for the next customer.

Neither of them paid much attention to the gangly youth who walked in. Perhaps if they'd bothered to look at him a bit sooner, they would have wondered why he was wearing such a heavy coat in such scorching hot weather. By the time Robert Naughton pulled a shotgun out from under that coat it was too late.

The first shower of metal hit Mohinder Cheema in the side of his chest. As he keeled over on the floor behind the counter, Naughton pointed and fired a second time right at his victim. But this time the fragments of shot missed most of their target except for Mohinder's fingers. Doctors later found loads of pieces of shot embedded in his hands.

Julie Cheema screamed as she watched Naughton standing over her husband with the gun. Naughton then turned and fled as her husband lay groaning on the floor. Julie Cheema rushed to his side. She looked down at his blood stained shirt, and could clearly see he was still very much alive. She tried not to look too disappointed. Then she left him there bleeding on the floor and looked outside at Naughton as he made off into the distance. Then she started sobbing.

'Oh my God. Mohinder. Oh my God.'

Two of the couple's children rushed down the stairs from the flat above. Julie stumbled to the phone and ever-so-slowly called the ambulance service. She didn't want them there too fast in case her husband stayed alive too long.

But Mohinder Cheema was still hanging on when the paramedics arrived on the scene. Julie had no choice but to hold her husband's hand in the ambulance as it rushed to a nearby hospital. She had a horrible feeling her husband was going to survive – and that would mean planning another hit all over again. This time they couldn't fail. The tears she shed that day were filled with disappointment not fear. She had willed her husband to die but he just wouldn't go that easily.

The shooting of Mohinder Cheema created quite a stir in the newspapers that week. So-called expert crime reporters on the national press wrote serious in-depth pieces on the Asian Mafia-style gangs that were believed to have gunned down the off-licence owner because he refused to pay protection money. Neighbours in Cromwell Road were said to be in deep shock about the shooting. Respectable Indian and Pakistani shopkeepers spoke in great detail about their run-ins with these notorious gangs. Even Julie Cheema voiced her determination not to bow down to these evil young criminals who'd so nearly taken away the life of her dearly beloved husband.

'I haven't paid and I won't pay. I work seven days a week and I won't hand over any of my hard-earned money,' she told one TV reporter.

And the headline in the *Daily Mail* summed it all up

perfectly: 'CORNER SHOP WIFE DEFIES THE MOBSTERS.'

Over in Charing Cross Hospital, west London, Mohinder Cheema underwent emergency surgery which involved the removal of one kidney, and had one of his fingers amputated. But at least Mohinder's brave battle to stave off the brutal Asian gangsters turned him into a hero in the local press. Mohinder Cheema was now a bit of a celebrity.

Mohinder even hired a team of bodyguards to protect him when he was released from hospital. He voiced public concern for his wife's safety back at the off-licence they owned. He insisted she didn't work alone on the premises. Julie Cheema couldn't help chuckling to herself realising she'd sparked off terror in the Asian community. Other killings and shooting of shopkeepers throughout west London were soon being linked to the Mohinder Cheema case.

But Julie Cheema remained determined to make sure her husband wasn't so lucky second time around, although hiring bodyguards would make her job far more difficult. She spent days scheming and plotting with her young friend Neil Marklew when her husband was in hospital.

'This time, you better make sure he dies,' she told Marklew.

As they discussed how to make sure it really did work, Julie stroked his youthful face and leaned over and kissed him full on the lips. That's when she knew he'd do anything for her.

'It has to be done as soon as he gets home. I don't want any of those bodyguards getting in the way.'

So, as Mohinder Cheema lay in a hospital bed, his wife Julie made love to Neil Marklew for the first time. The teenager was delighted to be taught some bedroom tricks by Julie. She was much more experienced than anyone he'd ever slept with before. He sat back and let her take complete control.

As she straddled his body in the bedroom of the home she still shared with her husband, Julie asked her young lover. 'You promise he won't miss this time?'

'Of course he won't. This time it will be done.'

Julie Cheema continued making love with her teenage boyfriend. She was looking forward to the day when she could call all those businesses her own. That would teach her husband to try and cut her out of his will. Throughout this time, Julie Cheema continued to convince her husband's family and the police that she had nothing whatsoever to do with the vicious attack on her husband. Julie had even taken him flowers and fruit as he lay in hospital linked up to heart monitors and drips. She was sorely tempted to pull them out of their sockets and just walk calmly away from that room. But Julie knew that all fingers would point to her. No, she had the perfect cover of those Asian gangs out to kill her defiant husband. It was obvious they'd come after him again.

Julie Cheema was delighted when doctors told her that her husband could go home on 3 October 1990 – six weeks after that shotgun attack in the off-licence. As she drove him back through west London she felt a twinge of nervous excitement building up inside. She kept telling him how glad she was that he'd been released from hospital. How relieved she was that he'd decided to hire minders. Mohinder Cheema looked at his wife in admiration. She really was bearing up to all the stresses and strains very well.

The journey back home took about 45 minutes, but Mohinder Cheema insisted on taking a look around his off-licence before going upstairs to their flat to recuperate. As he walked around the shelves, still in his dressing gown and slippers, inspecting the stock, she knew what a boring, mean old man he was. He didn't even trust her enough to let her carry on running the business without interfering. He wanted to know why they were short of stocks of certain brands of wine. She answered him sweetly because she knew that it wouldn't be long now.

Then Julie turned and saw the familiar figure of Robert Naughton approaching the shop. She walked round behind the counter and waited impatiently. Come on. Come on. Let's just get it over and done with.

Just like before, Mohinder Cheema didn't notice Naughton until it was too late. This time, he turned towards the gunman and looked over at his wife standing silently nearby. Mohinder Cheema knew at that moment she was behind it. The nervous expression on her lips gave it all away.

Robert Naughton blasted both shots close to his head this time. He couldn't fail. The shots hit Mohinder in the back of the head and the neck. There was no way he could survive them this time. The moment his body crashed to the floor of that off-licence he was already well on his way to being dead. Mohinder Cheema's 20-year-old son Sunil – who'd just walked into the shop – only realised what was happening when it was too late. If he'd been a few moments earlier he would have seen that look on his stepmother's face.

As Sunil rushed next door to a neighbour to raise the alarm, Julie Cheema leaned down and looked over her husband's body for the second time in less than two months. This time he was dead. A warm smile came to her lips and she stood up and walked towards the front of the shop, trying hard to force a sob and a tear to well up in her eyes. Mohinder Cheema lay in a pool of his own blood still wearing the Charing Cross Hospital dressing-gown he'd had on when he arrived at the shop just a few minutes earlier.

Julie Cheema was found guilty of murder and attempted murder when she appeared in front of a jury at the Old Bailey in July 1991. Her lover, Neil Marklew, and his friend Robert Naughton admitted murder and attempted murder. All three were given life sentences.

Detectives admitted that if it had not been for the testimony of Neil Marklew, Julie Cheema might never have been arrested. Her son Kismat, aged 18, was given three months' youth custody for conspiring to murder Mohinder Cheema.

Chapter Seventeen:

NUDE RUB-OUT

Santa Barbara, California, is a picturesque beachside paradise: miles and miles of pure white sand overlooking the Pacific Ocean. Even the pavements and streets are kept pristinely clean by a city council that insists on nothing but the best.

But just two hours' drive south of the city is the sprawling metropolis of Los Angeles with all its well-publicised problems. Local police in Santa Barbara are always on the look-out for troublemakers entering their little piece of heaven-by-the-sea. Yet behind its family-orientated image and wholesome exterior lies a seedy underbelly, typical of any seaside community from Brighton to Benidorm.

And, according to many locals, one of the most 'distasteful' elements that attracts the wrong sort of people is the notorious El Capitan beach just outside the city boundaries. This is where the home values and straight-laced beliefs of so much of Middle America give way to sleaze. In a nation where bare breasts are censored on prime-time television yet mass killings by gun-wielding teenagers are not uncommon. The El Capitan beach is a place that people refer to in hushed tones – it is, you see, a good, old-fashioned nudist beach.

Lots of nature lovers saunter down to the isolated beauty spot and strip off in a bid for the ultimate all-over tan. And, significantly, the majority of visitors to El Capitan are middle-aged citizens. The younger generation has always avoided the place like the plague. Many of them are appalled and disgusted by the middle-aged paunches and roasting flesh that have become a part of everyday life on El Capitan Beach. But then more than 70 per cent of America's population still goes to church every Sunday so perhaps it's not so surprising.

Phillip Bogdanoff and his pretty wife Diana were two such avid sun-worshippers. They loved making the short trip from their mobile home at the El Capitan Ranch Park right across the street to the beach. It was a dream come true for Phillip who had a healthy – some would say unhealthy – interest in examining the figures of nude beachgoers. His idea of a nice day out was to cast his gaze across the perfectly formed muscles and firm thighs of some of the beach's other regular visitors.

But then handsome, rugged, fun-loving 49-year-old engineer Bogdanoff kept himself in pretty good shape as well. He was proud of his own six-pack and relished the chance to strip off to his birthday suit on El Capitan beach. He'd already been a regular for many years when he started romancing an attractive fair-haired lady called Diana from nearby Colefax, California. Diana was working as a nursing aide at a nearby convalescence hospital when they first met in 1984. Both had suffered broken marriages, so they were understandably cautious at first and a four-year courtship followed. Diana already had children from her previous marriage, so there was no hurry to tie the knot.

In February 1989, Phillip and Diana married and moved to their dream location right opposite the most infamous nudist beach in Santa Barbara. So whenever they weren't working during that summer, Diana and Phillip would each pack a towel and set off across the street to the El Capitan Beach.

Diana told Phillip from the start of their relationship that said she didn't mind stripping off on the beach. He even suspected she enjoyed exhibiting her shapely body to the – mostly male – beach population. Phillip often caught healthily endowed guys staring at his wife's pert body. He'd smile at them before they could avert their gaze in embarrassment at being 'caught' peeping.

Sometimes Diana got so turned on she'd open her legs just a fraction whenever some of the more handsome beach-combers were watching at her eye level. She loved letting them see just a hint. Phillip knew what his wife was doing and even gave her behaviour his own bizarre seal of approval by observing the proceedings and *never* objecting to her behaviour.

But Phillip and Diana's favourite pastime was frolicking waist-high in the warm Pacific Ocean. Nude swimming was a hell of a refreshing way to pass the time. Diana and Phillip adored that feeling when the foamy surf enveloped them.

They used to say it was second only to making passionate love.

But on El Capitan Beach during those swelteringly hot summer months of 1989, Diana began letting her mind wander to other, less innocent things as she lay sunbathing in the nude. She'd sometimes close her eyes in the bright sunlight and think about the passionate affair she was having with the manager of the El Capitan trailer park across the street.

Diana Bogdanoff loved trailing her tongue down his neck and over his right nipple before biting gently into his soft skin. Then she moved back to his mouth and started probing deeper with her tongue. Running the tip right across his gums before pushing it deep into the full cavity of his mouth. Then she'd open her own mouth as wide as possible so that he could plunge his tongue deep into her throat. And Diana Bogdanoff never once considered her new husband, lying naked on the nudist beach just a few hundred yards away.

She'd first met the handsome stranger a few days earlier when he helped the couple move into their new home. But the moment he caught her looking him up and down they both knew they'd end up in bed together. Diana adored making hot, steamy love with a new rampant, virile man. Naturally, she liked to be on top most of the time. She also loved to tease and tantalise him, getting him really close to climaxing then letting go for a split second. It always made him beg for more.

But the greatest irony of all was that her husband of just a few months was lying on that nearby nudist beach ogling naked bodies, probably in just as excited a state. However Diana Bogdanoff preferred her new, young lover. She was willing and prepared to do anything to please him. As they lay there hot and sweaty after hours of lovemaking, she sat up and looked through the window to that nudest beach across the street and smiled to herself. Her husband got his pleasure watching naked bodies. She got her pleasure from performing the real thing. She realised her marriage was a sham – something she should never have undertaken in the first place. Now she needed a way out of it.

'If you wanted to kill someone, how would you do it?' she asked her secret lover as they nestled into each other's bodies.

He thought he was hearing things at first. Did she really just ask about killing someone moments after enjoying sex? But Diana Bogdanoff wasn't finished.

'Come on. A guy like you must know how to get someone killed.'

Still he didn't reply. The sex between them may well have been out of this world, but when she started talking about murdering her husband he began to wonder what sort of relationship he'd got himself into.

However Diana Bogdanoff wasn't deterred by her new lover's reluctance to respond. Her mind remained fully focused on this particular subject. Killing Phillip would solve a lot of problems, so she carried on.

'I thought about lacing his food with cocaine. D'you think that might work?'

'No way. He'd just end up getting high and havin' a great time.'

'What about poison? What would be the best brand to use?'

Diana's lover decided to play along with her 'game'. She couldn't possibly be serious. Could she?

'You wanna try getting some of that poison from those pencil trees that grow out near Morro Bay,' he said almost lightheartedly.

For the first time, he was starting to encourage her. He stopped in his tracks. Enough is enough. I must be crazy, he thought to himself. But Diana's mind was already set.

'Hey, that's a great idea. Will you come with me and help me find some of those trees?'

Her secret lover shook his head.

'No way. You must be crazy. Forget it. Get a divorce if you're so goddam unhappy.'

Diana got out of bed in a sulky silence, put her clothes on and headed out of the one and only door to that trailer. She was furious that he wouldn't help her. She'd have to find someone else who'd hatch a plan with her to kill her husband. That's when she decided to turn to her beautiful 18-year-old daughter Stephanie for help.

Diana Bogdanoff told Stephanie that husband Phillip had, 'beaten me and abused me more than I can handle. I gotta do something.' She was pretty convincing as a battered wife. The teenager sat, riveted by her mother's appalling revelations. How could her step-father be such a beast?

'You gotta help me kill him. It's the only way,' said Diana, close to crocodile tears.

'But Mom. That's murder you're talkin' about. Just get away from him. Just leave him.'

'But I've got nothing. If I leave him, I'll be out on the streets. If we kill him, at least I'll get to keep the house and all our money and things.'

'You're crazy mom.'

Like any self-respecting daughter, Stephanie was genuinely worried about her mother's safety at the hands of her supposedly brutal husband, but to murder him seemed rather drastic. Meanwhile Diana Bogdanoff sensed her daughter's sympathetic attitude. She decided to keep working on her until she had her 'on side'.

Over the next couple of months, Diana called up her daughter Stephanie at her home, 50 miles away in Bakersfield, and begged her to help her kill her 'brutal' husband. Initially she still got a definite 'No Way' response. But on the third attempt, Stephanie thought she sensed real panic in her mother's voice and gave in.

'I know this isn't right but if it's the only way then I guess we'll have to do it,' responded Stephanie.

Diana Bogdanoff was delighted. She'd grown to despise Phillip even more over the previous few months. The only time when she felt truly happy was when she closed her eyes and thought about her passionate affairs with other men. So, with daughter Stephanie on board, it was decided that one of her daughter's long-time admirers, a man called Raymond Stock, should carry out the execution, since he was still besotted with the shapely, long-legged teenager.

Stock had continually told Stephanie: 'There isn't anything I wouldn't do for you,' so now he was going to be put to the ultimate test.

It should be pointed out here that Stock's obsession with Stephanie was sweetened by the promise of $10,000 and part ownership of a house. As Stephanie snuggled up close to Stock on the settee at his home, she playfully stroked his thigh and said, 'I promise we'll be together afterwards and we're gonna have the time of our lives.'

Within hours the couple had stolen a car and switched its number plates, and were heading out towards Santa Barbara. Stephanie sat really close to Stock as they made the hour-long journey and talked in vivid detail about the plan to murder Phillip Bogdanoff: they'd go to the Bogdanoff mobile home, wait for Phillip to open the door and pump him full of bullets.

But as they approached the outskirts of Santa Barbara, Stock began suffering from an attack of guilty conscience. The idea of blasting Phillip Bogdanoff to death seemed all wrong. His hands started shaking, even though Stephanie was snuggling close to him as they drove. She kissed and licked his ear, neck and cheeks to try and help him relax. But the same thought kept going through Stock's mind: 'I'll go to hell if I do this.'

Just outside Santa Barbara, Stock announced to Stephanie he was pulling out of the hit. She was surprisingly calm and they turned the car around and headed back to Bakersfield in complete silence. When Stock dropped her off at her home, she'd already decided she'd never see him again. She'd have to find some other stupid man to do what he was told.

Just a few days later, Stephanie set out to persuade another of her admirers, Danny Kaplan, a neighbour from Bakersfield. He later recalled that there was something incredibly sexy about the teenager. When she nuzzled up to him and said she needed a favour, he couldn't resist helping her. Even after she'd explained the task, Kaplan took a huge gulp and decided to do it. He was hooked.

'I loved her so much I'd have done anything for her,' Kaplan said later. It was a familiar story. Stephanie had that sort of power over men. Kaplan didn't even object when Stephanie said her regular boyfriend – 21-year-old Brian Stafford – would be accompanying them on their mission to kill Phillip Bogdanoff. Kaplan still believed he'd be her only true love in the end.

A few days later, both men loaded shotguns and rifles into Kaplan's car and headed off towards Santa Barbara. This time the plan was to blast Phillip Bogdanoff to death as he drove alongside them on the motorway on his way back home from work. So by the time Kaplan, Stafford and Stephanie had arrived at Bogdanoff's workplace, all three were totally psyched up for the kill. They found a discreet vantage point overlooking the main entrance to the building and waited for Bogdanoff to come out.

Many hours passed. Then darkness fell and the three accomplices began to realise that maybe he wasn't at work that day. They got agitated and Kaplan started to question the entire plan for the first time.

'Let's call it a day. We'll have to think up a different way to do this,' he said nervously to the other two.

But Stephanie had other ideas. As the two men dropped their mini-armoury of weapons back in the boot of the car, she suggested a different way to kill her 'evil' stepfather. But Kaplan didn't want to know.

'I'm not going through with it. I want out of this,' he said.

Stephanie and her boyfriend Brian Stafford were angered by Kaplan's outburst.

'Hey, come on. You promised. We all agreed.'

Stephanie made it sound more like a playground dare than a mission to murder.

'No way. I cannot murder an innocent man.'

'But he's not innocent. He's beaten my mom. He deserves to die.'

'You don't know that for sure.'

Stephanie failed to dissuade Kaplan. They'd have to go back to the drawing board yet again. But nothing would make Stephanie give up. She ignored all her fears out of a fierce loyalty for her 'battered' mother. She believed the right opportunity would come along eventually. And boyfriend Stafford remained as passionate about Stephanie as ever. He'd do anything for her.

Just a few weeks later – on 21 September 1989 – Stephanie, Stafford and his great pal Ricky Rogers teamed up for what they hoped would be a third-time-lucky bid to murder Phillip Bogdanoff. This time the murder would be carried out on Bogdanoff's favourite El Capitan Beach.

That hot, sunny morning, the couple went on to the beach where they stripped off all their clothes and began topping up their all-over tans. El Capitan beach was very busy that day. The surf was crashing down forming huge slicks of bubbly froth on the sand as sun-worshippers lay completely naked on the strip of beach reserved exclusively for 'nature lovers'.

Diana and Phillip had settled in their favourite spot, just a few yards from the water's edge. It was the perfect location for him to cast his eyes across the beautiful suntanned oiled bodies that lay nearby soaking up the sunshine. Diana was more fidgety than usual. But then she did have rather a lot on her mind that day.

Instead of laying flat on her back as she normally did, Diana found herself sitting up with her knees close to her ample breasts as she watched the crowds from a distance. Watching. Waiting. Watching. Waiting. When Phillip looked across at Diana he noticed his wife's behaviour, but it never crossed his mind she was actually on the lookout for two fully clothed bodies. And the more Diana Bogdanoff looked out for her accomplices, the more she found herself ogling the naked men wandering in her immediate vicinity. One naked sun-worshipper even tried to give her the come-on because she'd been gazing past his right shoulder at two men loitering near the beach wall. At last the two would-be killers were in her sights. Reassured, she lay on her back and relaxed with a relieved smile on her face. It was just after 11am and the countdown to the end of Phillip Bogdanoff's life had begun.

A few minutes later, the shadow of two men loomed over Phillip and Diana Bogdanoff.

'Hey, man. You gotta joint?'

Phillip Bogdanoff squinted up at them through the strong sunlight.

'Excuse me? What did you say?'

'I said. You got some grass, man?'

Phillip was more a dry martini-type of character. Cannabis had never been on his menu.

'I don't smoke,' he replied nervously.

There was something about these two men he did not like. Diana didn't move an inch.

The two men then glanced at each other nervously. One of

them pulled a pistol out from under his shirt and pointed it straight at Bogdanoff, who tried to get up off the sand. Then the gunman pulled the trigger. The bullet ripped through Bogdanoff's cheek, spinning him off balance. That first wound was neat but ineffective. Brian Stafford leaned even nearer to his victim and fired again. This time Phillip Bogdanoff's head recoiled and he slumped back on to the sand. Limp. Naked. Bloody.

Then Diana Bogdanoff screamed in terror as she looked down at her own breasts and realised her dead husband's blood was splattered all over her naked body. The appalling reality of the murder sparked off plenty of real shock and emotion. She even felt bits of her husband's grist and tissue lodged in her long blonde hair.

Meanwhile gunman Stafford coolly and calmly put his pistol back inside his shirt and started running away from the couple with his accomplice. They heard Diana's cries for help and looked around for a moment to see her kneeling naked and bloody over the corpse of her husband – the man she'd ordered them to kill.

The secluded calm of that nudists' paradise was soon cruelly interrupted by dozens of police, paramedics, coroners' officers, press and onlookers desperate to get a glimpse of the naked guy blasted to bits on the beach in front of his wife. Just a few yards from where her husband had been killed sat the shaking figure of Diana Bogdanoff. Wearing a pullover covering her blood-spattered skin, the hysterical widow was being comforted by a tourist who just happened to be walking by moments after the shooting and had immediately offered her his jumper for cover.

'They shot my husband. They shot my husband.'

She just kept repeating the words over and over again. It was an impressive performance. No doubt she probably did feel a certain sense of bereavement and shock. Who wouldn't? A tearful Diana told police about the two strangers who came up to her husband and ended his life just because he told them he didn't smoke pot.

'Phillip didn't do anything,' she weeped. 'He didn't say anything to make them angry. He was just sittin' here.'

Detectives were genuinely baffled and all said later how sorry they felt for that poor, grieving widow. 'It was a senseless, cruel killing,' said one cop on the TV news that night. The town of Santa Barbara was soon virtually under siege from the media, and local residents genuinely feared that the mystery killers might strike again at any time.

But the only place Brian Stafford and his friend Ricky Rogers were heading was back to their homes in Bakersfield with the beautiful Stephanie snuggling between them on the bench seats of their old Chevy. Stephanie was delighted to have helped her poor, defenceless mother escape her nightmare marriage to a monster. And now she'd have a nice home to live in and a good income from his life insurance.

Back in Bakersfield, the murdering threesome broke open a few beers and proposed a toast at Stephanie's house.

'To a job well done.'

The beer bottles clinked and then Stephanie snapped on the TV to find a distressed Diana Bogdanoff pouring out her heart and soul to the news channels. The tragic widow shed numerous tears for the cameras, wrung her hands and gave a wonderfully convincing performance. The happy killers looked on and laughed. It had all gone even better than they'd expected.

A few minutes later Ricky Rogers left the house. Stephanie climbed into bed with her athletic lover Brian Stafford and they made the same sort of hot, passionate love that her mother prided herself on achieving every time she slept with yet another young stud. Like mother, like daughter.

Santa Barbara detectives Russ Birchim and Fred Ray were seasoned homicide cops who'd investigated just about every type of murder over the years. But the cold-blooded slaying of Phillip Bogdanoff truly baffled them. As one of them later recalled: 'No one gets killed over a joint. Certainly not on a nudist beach in broad daylight.'

Birchim and Ray soon concluded that Bogdanoff's grieving widow must have had something to do with it. But Diana Bogdanoff wasn't about to throw up her entire life by confessing to a crime she knew they couldn't pin on her, so she stuck rigidly to her story about the shooting of her loving husband. Even neighbours at the El Capitan Ranch Park had only good things to say about the Bogdanoffs: 'Nice couple'; 'Kept themselves to themselves'; 'A sweet pair'.

Detectives Birchim and Ray plugged away with composite sketches of the two killers based on eyewitness reports. Hundreds of likely-looking suspects were pulled in, interrogated and cleared over the following month. Birchim and Ray chewed over a few other possible theories. Maybe the two gunmen were a couple of screwballs high on dope. Perhaps it was all a case of mistaken identity. But whatever their suspicions about the case there was no hard and fast evidence to go on. The two cops were swimming around in the dark.

Then an anonymous caller phoned into a police informants' hotline in Bakersfield. The man said he had information about the nude beach murder in Santa Barbara. He said he'd met the two men who carried out the killing. 'I thought they were joking,' he told the police operator. 'Then I saw the newspaper reports and realised they'd really done it.' The tipster then named the people involved in the killing. The first name on his list was Raymond Stock, the man involved in the initial aborted attempt on the life of Phillip Bogdanoff.

When detectives called at Stock's home in Bakersfield he immediately confessed his involvement. The next one on the detectives' 'hit list' was Danny Kaplan. He had a similar story to tell. But this time he furnished the police with the names of Stafford and his pal Ricky Rogers as well as alleged ringleader Stephanie, daughter of Diana Bogdanoff. Kaplan also told officers how Stafford, Rogers and Stephanie came back to her apartment after the actual killing, bragging about what they'd just done.

'They were saying, "We did it. We did it. We blew the sucker away."'

Within days, the gang of three assassins had been rounded up. Then Diana Bogdanoff returned from a trip to visit relatives in Washington state and found a team of detectives waiting for her at Santa Barbara Airport. But she continued to stick rigidly to her story that she was innocent of any involvement in her husband's death.

Then cops had a big break when Diana's first husband

came forward and revealed that when the couple had divorced in 1980, she told him: 'You're lucky you're still alive. I tried to hire two men to kill you.' It then emerged that Diana Bogdanoff had been addicted to the idea of killing lovers and husbands for years. Was Phillip Bogdanoff the first time she'd really gone through with her murderous plans? Armed with that evidence the police arrested Diana Bogdanoff and charged her with first-degree murder.

In March 1991, at the Santa Barbara County Superior Court, Stephanie pleaded guilty to second-degree murder and received a 15-year-to-life sentence. Boyfriend Brian Stafford pleaded guilty to first-degree murder and got 33 years after agreeing to testify against Diana Bogdanoff. Ricky Rogers entered a plea of no contest to one charge of voluntary manslaughter. He was sentenced to no more than ten years in jail because he did not pull the trigger.

In May 1991, Diana Bogdanoff's second trial (her first one was abandoned as a mistrial because the jury couldn't agree a verdict) was held at the same courthouse. It took jurors just two hours to find her guilty of first-degree murder. She was also found guilty of planning the murder for financial gain and lying in wait for the killing to take place. Under those 'special circumstances' she was given an automatic life sentence without parole.

Chapter Eighteen:

SHOPPING FOR LOVE

Their eyes met across a crowded supermarket. At first, Cecilia Salazar did not even notice the look of lust from her work colleague. A few hours later, their hands brushed as they both busily restacked the shelves after closing time. Again, Cecilia Salazar had no idea of the effect she was having on her workmate.

Next day, Cecilia's secret admirer tried to catch a glimpse of her curvaceous figure at every opportunity. When the 42-year-old mother-of-two leaned down to pick up some tins of beans that had fallen on the supermarket floor, she looked up to find her co-worker, 23-year-old Maria Serrato, standing over her with both hands on her hips. The younger woman had a glazed look in her eyes – and she couldn't stop staring at Cecilia.

Maria wanted to turn her passionate fantasies about Cecilia into reality. She couldn't get Cecilia out of her mind and longed to be locked in an embrace with her. Maria Serrato was a striking-looking woman with long, flowing dark hair that was as thick as the black loom of the night. Her sparkling, dark, saucer-shaped eyes were constantly snapping around, searching for the love she never got as a child. Cecilia was precisely the opposite. She looked younger than her years and was a much softer, gentler woman with a motherly disposition. But all that made Maria even more attracted to her. Maybe she would provide a shoulder for her to cry on in times of need.

Back in that Los Angeles supermarket, the manager was just closing up the store when Maria noticed Cecilia slipping into the storeroom at the back of the shop to get changed before going home to her husband and children. Maria headed swiftly and silently after her. Seconds later, she entered the dark and shadowy storage room.

'Who's that?' Cecilia called out when she heard the door creak open.

'It's only me,' replied Maria.

Cecilia relaxed. She was worried it might have been that lecherous assistant manager who'd tried to maul her a few months earlier at the staff Christmas party. Through the shadows, Maria studied the outline of Cecilia's body as she stood there in a pair of pantyhose and bra while changing into a dress. Maria moved towards her.

'Maria, what's wrong?'

'Nothin',' replied the younger woman, who was just inches from Cecilia by this stage.

Maria looked deep into Cecilia's eyes before reaching out and stroking the back of her neck. Then she pulled the older woman towards her and their lips met. Soon their tongues were slurping hungrily into each other's mouths. Then Maria started trailing her mouth downwards.

After they'd made love, Cecilia told a friend that the lust between her and Maria was like no other sexual encounter she'd ever experienced in her life. When she finally got home later that evening to the apartment in nearby Burbank that she shared with her husband and two children, she was physically and emotionally drained. Her mind kept flashing back to the scene in that storeroom. She couldn't seem to shake free of those vivid scenes of lust and passion.

'What's wrong?' asked her husband, Jose, who worked long hours in a factory to help pay for the family's modest existence.

'Nothing,' replied Cecilia. But he knew she was lying.

Next evening, Cecilia and Maria couldn't continue their passionate affair in the storeroom because some of the other workers were also staying late to stack shelves. Maria was irritated that she couldn't seduce her older lover once again. She had been thinking about their sexual encounter virtually every minute of that day.

That evening, as Cecilia walked towards the supermarket exit, Maria ran after her, desperate for one longing kiss just to seal their love for one another. Cecilia pulled away as Maria grabbed her by the hair and tried to kiss her fully on the lips, too besotted to care who might see them.

Across the street, Jose Salazar was waiting in his car to pick his wife up. He watched in horror as his wife turned away from the younger woman and immediately realised that his instincts about his wife having a lover were correct – except that she was having an affair with another woman.

Cecilia and Jose sat in silence on the drive home. Jose, 37, was too shocked to say anything. This was the ultimate insult to his macho, Mexican pride. How could she want another woman? What had driven her into the arms of another female? It was sick and twisted and he was appalled. Then he decided he must act fast to save his marriage so he brought up the subject at dinner that night.

'I saw her with you.'

Cecilia tried to ignore the remark at first. But the wall of silence between them only confirmed her husband's worst fears.

'Have you made love to her?'

She nodded her head and broke down in tears. She knew the hurt must have been unbearable for him, but she had to unload her guilt to someone.

'I couldn't help it. I'm so sorry. I really am.'

And Cecilia meant every word she said. If anyone had ever suggested she'd have sex with another woman she would have laughed in their face. But Jose's priority was to guarantee that his wife would never sleep with another woman again.

'I want you to stay away from her. Never let her near you again. D'you understand?'

Cecilia nodded and solemnly promised to do as her husband wished. She had no intention of risking the break-up of her family. She just wished she could turn the clock back and wipe out the memories of those encounters with Maria forever.

Next day in the supermarket, Cecilia avoided going near

Maria for most of the morning. But she could feel the younger woman's eyes on her wherever she went in that supermarket. Eventually, Maria cornered Cecilia just before lunch break. Cecilia tried to tell her calmly that they could not see each other again.

But Maria snapped, 'I want you to myself. You are mine. Not his.' Clearly her obsession was not going to be that easy to ignore.

Cecilia ignored the remark and turned to walk away.

'You will be *all* mine one day,' screamed Maria.

Cecilia prayed that her lover would go away.

For the following week, Cecilia tried her hardest to avoid any contact with Maria. She went home in her supermarket uniform so she didn't have to visit that storeroom where their affair had started. She even resisted the temptation to look in Maria's direction whenever she appeared at one end of the supermarket while they were restacking shelves.

Then early one morning, Cecilia was up a ladder against a high shelf when Maria stopped below her and let her hand stroke the top of her lover's thigh. Cecilia looked down and snapped, 'Stop it, Maria. It's all over.'

'No, it isn't. I want you to myself. I need you.'

Cecilia sighed with anxiety and ignored Maria's outburst, she was beginning to realise that the younger woman would be very difficult to shake off. But she could never have guessed what lengths Maria was prepared to go to in order to have her to herself.

The two 15-year-old boys had been expert shots since the age of 12, thanks to their school-less lives on the mean streets of north Hollywood. So they weren't that surprised when Maria Serrato contacted them through a friend of her sister's.

'I want you to hit this guy. He's gotta die. If he doesn't, then I ain't payin' you a cent.'

The two youths looked at each other and shrugged their shoulders.

'How much?'

'One hundred dollars.'

'You kiddin' me?' said one of the teenagers.

'Take it or leave it.' Maria snapped. After ten minutes of haggling, the boys were convinced by Maria that it would be an easy hit, so they might as well do it for a hundred measly bucks.

A few days later, Maria picked the two boys up from their homes and drove them to Cecilia's apartment, parked up her truck and waited. After a few minutes, she spotted the unmistakable shape of the woman she wanted to make passionate love to emerge from the apartment and get into her own car to collect her husband from work.

'That's her. Now just wait here for her to return with her husband and hit him when they pull up.' There was a quiver in Maria's voice, but it wasn't nerves that were causing it. She just couldn't wait to make love to Cecilia again. I'll soon have you to myself, she thought. So Maria dropped the two boys outside the apartment block and drove around the corner to a spot where she could see everything, but would not be observed by them.

Jose Salazar was in a pretty good mood when his wife picked him up from work that evening. They seemed much happier than they had been for years. Strangely, the emotional upheaval of that affair with Maria had cleared the air between them. Now they were actually communicating together and even enjoying a rejuvenated sex life. Cecilia sometimes felt pangs of guilt about the whole business – especially since Maria's expert seduction of her had actually helped improve her sexual technique with her husband.

Neither Jose nor Cecilia noticed the two teenagers loitering on the worn-out patch of grass in front of their apartment block as they parked up that evening. And they certainly didn't see the semi-automatic .32-calibre gun hidden under one of their shirts. It was Cecilia who eventually saw them first approaching. But by the time they started pumping bullets into her husband, it was too late. The glazed look on the faces of those kids showed absolutely no emotion. They'd just earned themselves $100. They neither knew nor cared who their victim was.

Fifty yards away, Maria Serrato watched with cool satisfaction as Jose Salazar's body twitched and jerked when the bullets rained down on him. The boys came running around the corner and ripped open the passenger door to her truck. The threesome then sped away into the busy streets filled with commuters trying to get home after a hard day's work.

'How 'bout a bonus?' asked one of the kids hopefully as Maria carefully negotiated the queues of traffic on to the nearby motorway.

'No way. We made a deal.'

She handed over the $100 in crisp $20 notes. The boys didn't bother counting it. They could see it was the right amount.

That night, Maria lay awake in her apartment for hours. She couldn't stop thinking about how she'd soon be making warm, passionate love to Cecilia once again. She fantasised about all the things they would do to each other. She longed to have Cecilia there in the bed next to her – but at least she would not have to wait much longer.

A few weeks later, Cecilia returned to her job in the supermarket following her husband's brutal murder. She had no choice but to go back to work because someone had to feed the kids and pay the bills. And her lover Maria couldn't keep away from her. Within minutes, she trapped Cecilia in a quiet corridor and tried to push her against a wall to kiss her. Cecilia rejected her because her love for her husband had grown even more now that that he was dead.

When Maria told her proudly that she'd hired those boys to kill Jose, Cecilia was appalled. That lunchtime, she went to the detective investigating her husband's murder and informed them that Maria had commissioned the hit on her husband.

On 9 March 1993, Maria Serrato was found guilty of first-degree murder and sentenced to life in prison. The two schoolboys – not named because they were only 15 – were sentenced to youth authority until they turned 25 because they were too young to be given any heavier punishment.

'This is the most bizarre murder case I have ever been involved in,' said investigator Detective David Gabriel, of Burbank police, in Southern California. 'Never in all my years as a cop did I ever expect to be investigating such a killing. Mrs Salazar has admitted she had an affair with Serrato but she is now trying to put this whole nightmare behind her. She was sitting there in that truck when those boys pumped their bullets into her husband. It is something she will never ever be able to forget. Mrs Salazar has now moved to a secret address to try and put the pain and anguish of those awful events behind her.'

The two 15-year-olds arrested for the hit on Jose Salazar were freed less than two years later after serving their sentences in youth authority detention centres in northern California. They were paroled for good behaviour. Prison insiders said that the two boys were 'treated like heroes' because of the seriousness of their crime. 'They were considered tough guys compared with most of the other kids because of the severity of the case,' said one source.

As Detective Gabriel added, 'Those kids were under age and that's the law even if it might seem like a light sentence.'

SOME OF BRITAIN'S MOST INFAMOUS HITS IN RECENT YEARS

1. Martin Cahill – aka 'The General' – was gunned down by a professional shootist on 19 August 1993 in his Renault 5 in the Dublin suburb of Ranelagh. Just to ensure he had succeeded, the hitman fired five shots straight into notorious gangster Cahill with a .357 Magnum. Cahill had double-crossed other criminals and the IRA, so it was no surprise there was a bullet with his name on it.

2. Charlie Wilson. In 1990, the Great Train Robber was rubbed out by the pool of his £250,000 Marbella hacienda by Danny Roff. The hitman was himself on the run after escaping with associate Billy Edmonds from a British prison while serving 13 years for armed robbery. Wilson had double-crossed a big London syndicate during an illicit drugs deal.

3. Pat Tate, Craig Rolfe and **Tony Tucker** were shot dead in their Range Rover in an Essex field in December 1995. Their demise marked the end of one of the most notorious drug gangs in Britain, believed to be the one that supplied the ecstasy which killed tragic Essex teenager Leah Betts. Two men were later jailed for life for carrying out the killings.

4. **Pete McNeil** was shot at point-blank range by a motorcyclist outside his red-brick modern detached home in Hampshire on 10 February 1998. Millionaire-gangster-turned-police-informant McNeil – alias James Lawton – had been the supergrass in a $70 million cocaine heist that had connections with the Medellin drug cartel in Colombia.

5. **Keith Hedley** was killed by alleged bandits on his yacht *The Karenyann* in Corfu in September 1996. Kent-based Hedley, 56, was a suspected money launderer who was mown down by the so-called pirates when he tried to stop them stealing his dinghy.

6. **Kevin Whitaker** was a drug dealer killed by Pat Tate (see above) in the autumn of 1995, when he was forced to snort large quantities of a substance called Ketamine. Vets use Ketamine to tranquillise horses before castration but it is also used as a narcotic and is known in the underworld as 'Special K'. Whitaker's killers went on to pierce his groin with a syringe and pumped a deadly concoction of poison into his blood. They then dumped his body in a ditch near Basildon, Essex.

7. **John Marchall** was found shot dead in his black Range Rover in Sydenham, south London, in May 1996. Marchall,

34, also knew notorious ecstasy dealer Tate. Tattooed Marchall had earlier vanished from his £250,000 home at Little Burstead, Essex, after telling his family he was going to meet 'business contacts'.

8. Donald Urquart was shot in a London street in 1992. Urquart was a well-known London money launderer. It transpired that the gun used to kill him was supplied by a policeman-turned-gun-dealer, who later committed suicide. Urquart had been accused by other criminals of swindling them out of money during a huge, multi-million-pound money laundering scam.

9. Tommy Roche was killed in almost identical circumstances to those of the man he often 'minded', Donald Urquart. Roche, 42, was shot three times after stopping in a lay-by near Heathrow Airport on 21 June 1993. As a teenager, Roche had even worked for the Krays. He was a suspected police informant.

10. Nick Whiting was stabbed nine times and then shot twice with a 9mm pistol in 1990. Surveyors carrying out preliminary work for a new theme park at Rainham Marshes, Essex, stumbled upon Whiting's body hidden in undergrowth. He'd handled much of the gold stolen from the notorious Brinks-Mat robbery in the mid-Eighties.

11. Stephen Dalligan was shot six times in the Old Kent Road in 1990. Dalligan, 27, was the brother-in-law of Brinks-Mat robbery suspect Tony White. Although detectives insist he refused to help with police investigations, it is widely believed that suspicions about his involvement with the police led to his death.

12. Daniel Morgan was found with an axe embedded in his skull in a south London car park in 1987. The one-time police detective had been working as a private eye investigating police corruption when he was murdered. No one was ever arrested for the killing and there have been rumours in the south-east London underworld that a group of crooked policemen clubbed together to pay a hitman to wipe out Morgan.

13. Daniel 'Dannyboy' Valliday was at first thought to have died in a road accident, but the Ulster drugs baron was actually the victim of a clever assassin who made his death look like a hit-and-run. Valliday was so notorious that the IRA had ordered him to leave Ulster because of his outrageous drug deals. His killer was never found.

CONTRACT KILLERS

1. Danny Roff and **Billy Edmunds** were the successful hit-team behind the death of Charlie Wilson in Marbella. However, Wilson's criminal associates finally got their revenge when Roff was himself shot dead outside his home in Wanstead Road, Bromley, Kent, in March 1997. Roff was executed as he arrived home in his Mercedes. Two masked gunmen shot him at least five times in the head and chest before escaping in a stolen van. Meanwhile, Roff's accomplice in the Wilson hit in Spain – Edmunds – remains on the run from both criminals and police.

2. Jeremy Debonnaire arranged his own murder rather than face a painful, lingering death from cancer. He paid two men £3,000 to make his death appear like a botched burglary at his detached bungalow in Bearstead, Kent, in August 1997. His death must surely be one of the most bizarre contract killings in criminal history.

3. Pat Tate was probably Essex's most notorious E dealer when he decided to save the cost of hiring hitmen to wipe out business rivals by personally killing at least three criminals in an orgy of death that, not suprisingly, ended in his own brutal demise in his Range Rover in December 1995.

4. Terry Bewdley was paid to kill Bob Wignall in 1992 by his cheating wife Sandra, who even gave hubby Wignall oral sex in his car in a lay-by in Surrey to ensure that hitman Bewdley could walk up and kill Wignall when he was at his most defenceless. A hefty life insurance policy was at stake.

5. Bob Bell shot and killed businessman Terry Daddow on his own doorstep in a sleepy East Sussex village. Bell was hired by Daddow's wife, Jean, and her drug-dealing son, Roger Blackman. They were angry at Daddow's meanness and obsessed with getting a share of his life insurance payout.

CONTRACT KILLER FILMS

Leon (1995): By the mid-Nineties, even hitmen on the big screen had hearts of gold, and this one – played superbly by French actor Jean Renoir – makes you question your own morals.

Grosse Point Blank (1996): Brilliant low-budget movie, starring John Cusack as a hitman who goes back to his old school's reunion.

Pulp Fiction (1995): Tarantino's homage to the B movies of the Fifties provides audiences with Travolta and Samuel L Jackson as the two most bizarre hitmen you'll ever meet.

The Killer (1989): John Woo's bloodfest that many believe was the best movie he ever made, despite a big-budget Hollywood career in the Nineties.

Fargo (1996): The Coen Brothers' finest film, in which two bumbling hitmen make a balls-up of killing the wife of a twitchy used-car salesman.

Red Rock West (1992): Grossly underrated movie in which Nicholas Cage finds himself mistaken for a hitman, played brilliantly by cowboy Dennis Hopper.

The Hit (1984): A supergrass hiding in Spain is sought by two London gang executioners. Worth a look just to see Tim Roth in dark, sombre pre-*Reservoir Dogs* mood.

The Killers (1946): In a small, sleazy town a gangster – Burt Lancaster – waits for two assassins to kill him. This is the original film noir based on an Ernest Hemingway short story and it's brilliant! It also spawned a brutal remake intended for TV called ***The Killers*** (1946), starring Lee Marvin as one of the shootists and featuring Ronald Reagan in his last role before hitting the political trail.

Kill Her Gently (1958): Little-known low-budget B special about a madman who hires two convicts to murder his wife.

Other Books by Wensley Clarkson

Dog Eat Dog
Hell Hath No Fury
Like a Woman Scorned
Love You to Death, Darling
Mel
Tom
Slave Girls
Doctors of Death
Deadly Seduction
Death at Every Stop
The Mother's Day Murder
Shooting from the Hip
Back in Character
Public Enemy Number One
Sting
Killer on the Road
Gangsters
Hitman
Caged Heat
The Railroad Killer
The Boss
The Good Doctor
Child's Prey
The Babyface Killer
Rio!
The Mother from Hell
Hit 'em Hard
Inside the Cage